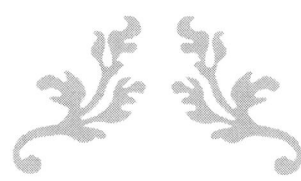

CULTURE CLASH

Seeing the Invisible

BO SALISBURY

Culture Clash   *Seeing the Invisible*

Visit Kingdom Culture International at: http:/KingdomCulture.life

Culture Clash: Seeing the Invisible   by *Bo Salisbury*

Copyright @ 2019 by Bo Salisbury. All Rights Reserved.

Cover design by Christopher Negron

Published by *Kingdom Culture Media*

This book and parts thereof may not be reproduced in any form, stored in a retrieval system or transmitted in any form by any means (electronic, mechanical, photocopy, recording or otherwise) without prior written permission of the author, except as provided by United States of America copyright law.

All Scriptures are from the NKJV, New King James Version Copyright @ 1982 by Thomas Nelson, Inc. Used by Permission. All Rights Reserved.

ISBN 9781694844521

First printing   October 2019

25 24 23 22 21 20 19

 5 4 3 2 1 12 11 10

Printed in the United States of America

Culture Clash   *Seeing the Invisible*

To the next generation of giant slayers God is raising up in the earth, to the young lions developing in your den, to the next wave of apostolic leaders being groomed for an earthshaking ministry, to turn the world upside-down...

Never settle for less than what Jesus died to give you!

Culture Clash *Seeing the Invisible*

Culture Clash *Seeing the Invisible*

Table of Contents

Introduction 11

Momentum Shifting, Building & Sustaining 15

Momentum & Fulfilling Destiny 17

Valuing Truth at All Costs 18

Inheritance 19

Can These Bones Live? 20

New Songs from Heaven 21

House of Prayer 22

Cookie-Cutter Christianity 23

Pray Without Ceasing 25

Divine Relationships 26

Diversity in Relationships 26

Rejecting Reality 28

Culture Clash 29

Apostolic Order 30

Adolescent Pastors 31

Culture Clash *Seeing the Invisible*

Giving Without Strings   31

Validation   32

Putting the Pieces Together   33

Mega Churches   35

God is So Cool!   38

Responding to Discernment   38

Frame your World with your Words   39

Your Words are Weapons of His Choice   40

Too Much of a Good Thing   41

God Knows what He's Doing   42

Before you Leave your Church   42

Transferring Grace   45

Defining Relationships   45

Equip the Saints   46

Baking Bricks for Pharaoh   47

Sowing & Reaping   48

Success of the Church   48

Qualifications of Leaders   49

You Can Do It!   50

Detoxification   51

Culture Clash   *Seeing the Invisible*

Church Hurt   52

Two Kinds of Signs   53

Five-fold Grace   56

Apostolic Music   58

New Wine Skins   58

The Power of a Reminder   59

Fulfilling Prophetic Words   59

The Reformers are Coming   60

Charis-maniacs   61

True Spirituality   62

Codependence   62

True Honor   64

Toxic Relationships   66

Preaching a Custom-Fit Word   67

Religious Mentalities   70

Pressing into the Kingdom   70

Rethinking Offerings   71

Manipulators vs. Motivators   75

Spiritual Footnotes   77

Discipling Nations   78

Culture Clash   *Seeing the Invisible*

Healing the Hurts   79

Apostolic & Prophetic Pendulum   79

Accessing Grace   80

My Grace is Sufficient for You   81

Prayers that Don't Ask for Stuff   82

The Priority of Prayer   82

Hypocrisy   83

Double for your Trouble   84

Contend for Unity   85

Let My People Go!   86

True Contentment   87

Paradigm Upgrade   88

Handling Dysfunctional Saints   89

Ministry Ain't Glamorous   90

The Hindrance of Money   93

Rebellion in Leaders   94

Prophecy & Relationships   95

Dominion is a 'We' Thing   96

Territorial Apostles   98

Pendulum Swings   99

Culture Clash   *Seeing the Invisible*

Greater Level of Unity   100

Investing in Those you Don't Know   101

Discerning Different Relationships   102

Becoming a Finisher   103

Apparent Parent Abuse!   104

The Next Apostolic Wave   105

Apostolic Remnant   107

The Power of Light   108

Vulnerability   109

Spiritual Abortion & Euthanasia   110

The Responsibility of Senior Leaders   112

Community in the Local Church   114

Terrorism   115

His Still Small Voice   116

Fight Fire with Fire   117

Desire to Prophesy   117

Show some Mercy   118

Calibrated with Kingdom Culture   119

Joshua-type Relationships   120

True Spiritual Fathers   121

Culture Clash *Seeing the Invisible*

Immature Leadership   122

My Take on Titles   123

Jezebel   124

Spiritual Burnout   125

13 Roles of an Apostolic Builders   128

No Cookie-Cutter Apostles   129

Apostolic Progression   130

Unspoken Sermons   132

The Wealth of the Wicked   132

Dealing with Giants   133

Follow the Blueprint   134

Divine Purpose   135

Less is More   135

Too Deep   136

Politics & Religion   137

Mature Discernment   138

Conclusion   140

Biography   141

Kingdom Culture Exchange   143

Contact Info   153

Introduction

Paradigms are defined as "outstandingly clear ways of thinking" and they are powerful! They can be based on the truth that prevails in the Kingdom of heaven or they can be based on earthly cultures that contradict what God believes. The latter are difficult to penetrate, even with potent truth. That's because we're conditioned to protect certain beliefs with philosophies and traditions of men that reinforce our core priorities.

Even Jesus had a challenging time trying to shift the paradigm of his closest disciples. The Scriptures were clear that God would send a Messiah to deliver the Jewish people from oppression, but after 430 years of silence from the last OT prophet to the first NT prophet, many traditions and philosophies developed and thus distorted what the Scriptures clearly said about Jesus.

That's why when Jesus showed up, even though he fulfilled many specific prophecies about himself, the majority of people had a difficult time receiving him as their Messiah. He just didn't match what they came to believe about their coming deliverer.

The Pharisees and Sadducees emphatically rejected the notion that Jesus was their Messiah but some people believed he was "the One," so much that they tried to make him king.

Culture Clash   *Seeing the Invisible*

But Jesus would have nothing to do with that. That's because His Kingdom was not of this world. That reality clashed with the existing paradigm that caused people to believe that they would rule with world under the leadership of Christ. That's the thought process behind James and John asking Jesus if they could sit on his *"left and right hand in his kingdom."*

Even after 3 ½ years of full-time on-the-job training with Jesus himself, the old paradigm in the 12 disciples was still intact. We know this to be true because just before Jesus ascended to the Father, they asked him, *"Lord, will you at this time restore the kingdom to Israel?"* Jesus refused to answer their question and simply redirected their focus on their assignment, knowing it would take the power of the Sprit on the Day of Pentecost to deliver them from their old way of thinking.

Before **Acts 2**, the disciples were extremely competitive because their paradigm was shaped by earthly values. But after **Acts 2**, you see a dramatic shift in their actions. Twelve apostles began to function as one to lead the church forward. What happened? The power of the Spirit combined with the truth Jesus spoke to them to dismantle an old paradigm that was hindering their progress. And moving forward, the apostles began to deliver others from the paradigms that hindered them from accepting Christ and from progressing in the Kingdom of God.

The 21st century church has a tremendous need for our paradigms to be reshaped according to Kingdom culture. Much like the first century Jews, our beliefs are often

Culture Clash   *Seeing the Invisible*

reinforced by philosophies and traditions of men, causing us to see things in a certain light, but at the same time to reject anything that challenges or contradicts our current paradigm.

This book is a combination of revelation, wisdom and spiritual understanding that comes from an apostolic perspective, not prevailing religious mentalities. The purpose of this book is to challenge what you believe so what you see becomes congruent with Kingdom realities. Your life will never change until your mind is renewed. And your mind won't be renewed unless you receive the spirit of wisdom and revelation to upgrade your thinking.

It's my prayer that these compact nuggets of truth will help you see what you've never seen before, do what you've never done before and become everything God wants you to be! With this in mind, my suggestion is that you take your time reading this book. Don't rush through it or you will sabotage the process of renewing your mind. Read each segment and take a few moments to meditate on what you just read. Perhaps take a few minutes to pray about things, asking God to adjust your thinking, to activate these truths in your life and to inspire a new level of productivity in your ministry.

Ultimately, God wants to clarify our vision so he can empower us for ministry. He wants us to see the invisible so we can do the impossible! And as we find our place in the body of Christ and in the world, we will become an unstoppable force to be reckoned with. We will become the invincible body of Christ that will turn the world upside-down once again! Let Your Kingdom Come!!

Culture Clash   *Seeing the Invisible*

Bo Salisbury

Kingdom Culture International

CULTURE CLASH

Seeing the Invisible

-If you exercise more faith to develop your gift than your character, you are setting yourself up for failure.

-Knowing when to let someone in your world is important. If you let people in that you shouldn't, the waters of your soul will get muddied. Use discretion with your doors.

If you don't let someone in that you should, you'll miss out on great refreshing. Windows of opportunity aren't there forever.

MOMENTUM SHIFTING, BUILDING & SUSTAINING

1. When things aren't going well, whether that means your strength is waning, you give into temptation, the trials of life are vexing you or you are being persecuted, go to God <u>immediately</u>! Timing is crucial! The longer it takes to recognize your need for God's grace in your situation and the longer you wait to access it by faith, the deeper you will find yourself sinking into a rut. Don't wait until your spiritual gas tank gauge is on empty to go to the gas station. Be filled every day throughout the day with His Spirit!

Culture Clash   *Seeing the Invisible*

2. Don't wait until you're in desperate need of God's intervention to build a spiritual reservoir of God's wisdom today will pay off when difficulty arises tomorrow. Never forget your need for daily bread that Jesus taught his disciples to pray for.

Make it a daily habit to develop your spirit man through personal prayer, the Word and worship. And please don't depend on the next church service to get you through. "<u>Build yourself up</u> *in your most holy faith, praying in the Holy Spirit.*" Don't look to others to do for you what you should do for yourself.

3. Don't get overconfident and forget that you need others too. Recognizing and engaging in God-ordained relationships for your life is crucial to building and sustaining spiritual momentum. Praying for the right people to come into your life, developing healthy relationships and working through conflict are absolute musts.

If you neglect relationships you will find yourself in a cave like Elijah, wanting to give up. Exiting toxic relationships and knowing when to make adjustments in dysfunctional relationships are also very important to spiritual momentum. You can't sustain forward movement when certain people in your life aren't moving in the same direction or at the same pace as you.

4. Daily decision-making can make a bad day worse or a good day better. Reacting rashly in frustration or fear can definitely compound problems, but taking a step back, calming down, asking God for wisdom and then making the

best decision possible can get you back on the right path. Doing the best you can with the resources you have while believing God for favor and provision will go a long way. How you manage your time, money and other resources will detract or add to your momentum.

5. Remaining teachable and humble positions you for sustained momentum. Always asking God to teach you, change you and use you will ensure your awareness of what He is saying and doing in your life. And by all means, read and learn from others.

And by the way, it doesn't need to be all spiritual stuff. We live in a natural world and spiritual world at the same time, so realize your need for improvement and do something to become better prepared for what God has called you to do. When you stop learning, you stop growing. And when you stop growing, you invite old habits back into your life.

MOMENTUM & FULFILLING DESTINY

-Stopping negative momentum as soon as possible, and initiating and sustaining positive momentum are keys that will enable you to minimize damage during difficult times and capitalize on the good times. But with faith in God's ability to turn things around, He will even cause great things to emerge out of the rubble of tragedy!

Just don't make things worse than they already are by making decisions you regret later. This feeds into negative momentum. Hit the brakes on negative momentum and put the pedal to the metal with positive momentum! God is on your side. Lean on His wisdom and grace, and you will see things move forward!

VALUING TRUTH AT ALL COSTS

-The market is much greater for those who tickle ears than for those who teach truth these days. There's even a much higher demand for those who will bless you with external demonstrations of the Spirit than for those who will challenge you with the internal workings of the Spirit that take place when hardcore truth is preached.

The question is whether you will cater to the desires of your flesh or prioritize what God is saying and doing in and through your life. What would be different if money were removed from the equation? What messages would rise to the surface and what messages would take a backseat? How would things change if truth were valued above your feelings?

Perhaps if our hearts would return to wanting to please the Lord at all costs instead of making a god out of money or our feelings, we would gravitate toward those who truly want to see Christ formed within us. Our spiritual taste buds would change. We would lose our appetite for anything that is candy-coated and crave what will transform our minds and hearts.

May God raise up a generation of leaders who have the interests of those they serve in mind, not just what they can get out of them. MONEY.

May God raise up a generation of believers who will "turn the channel off," away from those who simply aim to tickle

Culture Clash   *Seeing the Invisible*

their ears and make them feel good. Also turning away from those who condemn and control. Let God's people gravitate towards spiritual parents who truly aim to raise them up into maturity, so the ceiling of the fathers becomes the floor of the sons!

-Less is sometimes more. If we would exchange our "busy-ness" in ministry for quality time ministering to God and intentional living in response to the leading of the Spirit, we would get much more accomplished for the Kingdom of God.

-Discovering who you really are is only possible by revelation from the Spirit. You can try to be something you're not, but your purpose won't be fulfilled and neither will you be.

INHERITANCE

-*"...as long as the heir is a child, he is no different from a slave, although he owns the whole estate..."* **Galatians 4:1**

Inheritance is <u>available</u> through relationship but <u>accessible</u> only through maturity.

-No matter what you say on social media, somebody is going to think you're talking about them. By all means, don't use social media to address personal issues. But don't be afraid to share something that could benefit others.

Culture Clash   *Seeing the Invisible*

-Don't disqualify yourself from God's blessings based on your performance. You are blessed because of faith, not perfection.

CAN THESE BONES LIVE?

-The beginning of **Ezekiel 37** paints a hopeless picture of a humungous pile of dry bones in a valley. They're actually the remains of the Jewish army that was completely obliterated in a war. Not a single survivor. Nobody was left to conduct funerals, hence tens of thousands of dry bones just decaying out in the open after their flesh was eaten by vultures. I know, kind of a graphic description of a totally hopeless situation! But God!!

God caused the prophet Ezekiel to get a close-up view of this hopeless situation and then asked him a riveting question: "*Can these bones live?*" Ezekiel most likely thought the answer was "No" but because God presented the idea as a possibility, he presumed God must know something that he didn't. That's why he responded "*Oh Lord God, You know.*"

But God put the ball back in Ezekiel's court by telling him to "*Prophesy to these bones to hear the word of the Lord.*" As Ezekiel prophesied bones aligned properly with each person, ligaments and tendons began forming, vital organs instantly developed and skin covered them all! But they were still not breathing. Then God told Ezekiel to prophesy again, this time to the breath to come into them. And AS he prophesied, the entire army was revived and stood on their feet!

We've all been in hopeless situations before, and some of you are there right now. God wants you to agree with His word and declare with your mouth your own deliverance, healing and provision! There is power in your words!! What may appear to be hopeless is a setup for a miracle from heaven, but God needs your cooperation and participation in your own breakthrough. He needs you to agree with Him by holding on to your faith, by exercising your faith. Then and only then will your breakthrough manifest!! Hold on! Your new season is just around the corner!!

NEW SONGS FROM HEAVEN

-I love when a new song from heaven starts resonating in my heart. It's as if my spirit tunes into a spiritual frequency and I begin listening to music in my heart's radio. I occasionally wake up to new songs this way and they keep popping up throughout the day when I least expect it.

Sometimes I hear them in my dreams and then record them after I awake. I've written hundreds of songs this way in response to what I hear internally. So really, I'm not a songwriter. I simply echo what lives beyond the world we live in.

HOUSE OF PRAYER

-Immediately after Jesus made a whip he went into the temple, turned over the tables and seats of the money changers, poured out their money on the floor and drove out

Culture Clash   *Seeing the Invisible*

the oxen and sheep. Then the blind and lame came to him in the temple and were healed.

We will see Kingdom results in our ministries when we allow Jesus to set Kingdom order in our midst.

Did it cross your mind how blind people were able to see to find Jesus in the temple? Ever thought of how lame people came to Jesus? Didn't have wheelchairs back then! Perhaps the blind carried the lame as the lame told the blind where to go!!

Jesus' main frustration was that his house was supposed to be a house of prayer but the religious leaders made it a den of thieves. Leaders were supposed to help connect people to God and one another, but they were taking advantage of them.

The "house" of prayer is a <u>household</u> of prayer, the family of God. We gather with our spiritual family to worship God together, to know Him more, to become more like Him and to minister to one another.

When leaders get their stuff in order, becoming servants of God's people instead of lording over them, this paves the way for God's people to experience a divine exchange with heaven in the midst of our gatherings. The weakness of the blind will be supplemented by the strength of the lame and vice versa.

May God bring order to His house so it can be the household of prayer it is meant to be. That way God will be glorified and we will fulfill our purpose to represent Him well in the earth.

Culture Clash   *Seeing the Invisible*

-When Jesus sent his disciples on mission, he told them *"Freely you have received, freely give."*

If rivers of living water aren't flowing freely through you, perhaps you're not consistently drinking living water in your prayer life or perhaps you're not drawing water from the wells around you.

You can only give what you have received. And it's your responsibility to keep the flow going by dealing with blockages in your receiving and giving.

COOKIE-CUTTER CHRISTIANITY

-Besides opening up presents under the tree, my favorite thing about Christmas as a child was eating a huge variety of Christmas cookies. OK, so that's still pretty high on my list today. From sugar cookies with icing to buckeyes to molasses cookies, I just couldn't get enough. Chase that down with a half-gallon of milk and I was in heaven! My taste buds were extremely satisfied with the variety of sweet flavors invading my mouth.

What I learned was that the Christmassy-shaped cookies were actually formed by cookie-cutters. In other words, my grandma didn't take her sweet time carving out each Christmas tree, snowman and candy cane. They were products of a Christmas cookie "franchise" that duplicated the original design. I used to think grandma slaved away in the kitchen for days on end until I found out the truth.

Culture Clash   *Seeing the Invisible*

It dawned on me the other day that the church is suffering from "cookie-cutter Christianity" syndrome. Although God has gifted His church with a multiplicity of spiritual gifts, many churches resemble a tray-full of sugar cookies or a bowl-full of chocolate and peanut butter buckeyes. We have the tendency to elevate certain gifts above others, only to duplicate our priorities and preferences into the next generation, regardless of how God has gifted them.

Paul told the Corinthian church *"imitate me, just as I imitate Christ."* This verse tells it all. Paul's exhortation is NOT for people to copy him. It is for people to take note of how he follows Christ and to do the same. When our eyes are focused on our leaders and not on Christ, we can become byproducts of a church culture instead of allowing the specific gifts God has placed within us to blossom. In fact, if we happen to be in a church environment that doesn't celebrate the gifts God has deposited within us, our gifts will be suppressed and we will be frustrated.

The church is diametrically opposed to business franchises like McDonald's. In other words, discipleship isn't the process of duplicating yourself in the lives of others. It is the process of helping people connect directly to Christ, discover their own God-given gifts and how they can engage them to fulfill their specific purpose. If we busied ourselves with this type of discipleship, the kingdom of God would forcefully advance to every corner of the earth. But as long as we are more concerned with making sure people believe and act just like us, we will continue to compete in the Christian marketplace for our piece of the pie.

Culture Clash   *Seeing the Invisible*

Let's appreciate every gift under the tree. (Every Spirit-endowed gift that is a result of the cross) And yes, let's appreciate the diversity of Christmas cookies too!

PRAY WITHOUT CEASING

-I used to think "*praying without ceasing*" meant that we should pray 24/7 or at least have constant inner communion with Him. Although I do believe the latter, I really believe the intent of this scripture is to encourage us to beware of anything that tries to hinder us from spending the time with the Lord that we need to, from freely communicating with Him and from hearing everything He wants to speak to us.

Anything that challenges open communication from our heart to His and from His heart to ours needs to be immediately contended with! We need to be aware when our spiritual strength is low and get that replenished through seasons of strong prayer. We need to discern when we are under spiritual attack so we can press in to a place of freedom in God once again. We need to respond to times of temptation and persecution by retreating to the Lord for His protection and refreshment in His presence.

We often wait entirely too long to respond to the weak condition of our spirit, long after our flesh or the enemy takes us far away from that place of peace in Him He desires us to abide in! Guard your relationship with God. Don't allow your prayer life to cease being what it is meant to be. What it used to be! Press in and the Lord will rebuild the strength and sensitivity of your spirit once again.

Culture Clash   *Seeing the Invisible*

DIVINE RELATIONSHIPS

-I see an acceleration of **Ezekiel 37** happening in this generation, divine connections for Kingdom purpose. There is a special grace for relationship building and adjustments in this season for those who are committed to God's Kingdom agenda more than their personal endeavors. Who you truly are in the spirit will be unveiled to those who God wants to connect to you. If you're trying to prove your identity, you've stepped out of grace. You have nothing to prove, just abide in His grace.

See others for who they really are, not who they used to be and not what they may appear to be on the outside. That way you will be able to connect on a deeper level, a place where God can orchestrate relationships to serve His agenda. Recognize what God is doing beneath the surface and cooperate with His plan, and you'll see in reality the fruit of what God is birthing right now in the spirit!

DIVERSITY IN RELATIONSHIPS

-The Kingdom of God is not limited to our myopic view of spiritual relationships. Far too many relationships have been labeled father-son relationships when in fact they were meant to be something slightly or altogether different. And when relationships are mislabeled, the tendency is to try to jam a square peg in a round hole which only produces frustration, not fulfillment. Yes, you need a father but you could also use multiple uncles and big brothers to help form a well-balanced

Culture Clash   *Seeing the Invisible*

team of counselors in your life that serves as a safety net, primarily because of the diversity of perspectives they have from the Lord.

Trust me, putting all your eggs in one basket is more dangerous than you think, especially in light of **I Cor. 13:9** "*We know (see) in part and prophesy in part.*" You do not have the mind of Christ, WE do! That's why you can't be an island and be successful. Nor should your protective covering come from only one person. And if they demand that they alone can speak into your life, run for cover!! You have a jezebel spirit on your hand isolating you for ungodly control, using you for their advantage.

Read your Bible. Every local church had multiple elders. Believers weren't given the luxury of choosing their favorite and discarding the rest! Allow the Lord to bring people into your life and also allow Him to define who they are to be to you and vice versa. This shouldn't be an all-or-nothing thing. And if people think otherwise you might want to rethink whether God is putting them into your life in the first place. Might just be a wolf in sheep's clothing. Just sayin'! Judge people by their fruit, not their lofty promises and vain flattery.

-I don't know about you, but I'd rather lose my life at least attempting to fulfill my dream, than wonder what could've been as I rot in the decay of regret and misery!

REJECTING REALITY

Culture Clash   *Seeing the Invisible*

-It's amazing to see just how dysfunctional relationships have become these days due to the power of deception, soul ties, ungodly control and insecurities, all of which have their root in neglecting to deal with truth honestly. We have the tendency to reject the reality that is before us if we don't like it, and replace it with what we want to be true. We can easily convince ourselves that something is true when it isn't, simply because it makes us feel better.

If we don't like our situation, we ignore it or replace it with something that is easier to deal with. This is the result of our society conditioning us to do whatever makes us happy, without regard to the fact that if we don't deal with life head-on, it will come back to bite us. Ignoring our problems or trying to medicate them away with drugs, alcohol, sexual fantasy, eating or even shopping will not solve anything. It will just make things worse.

-True freedom is not the ability to do what you want, it's the ability to be who God intended you to be without bondage or limitation.

-As long as we are more influenced by the world than the Word, we will be powerless to advance the Kingdom of God in our society.

CULTURE CLASH

Culture Clash   *Seeing the Invisible*

-Contrary to popular opinion, Jesus didn't die for our sins so we could go to heaven one day. He died for our sins so heaven could come to us! The good news of the Kingdom of God is not that we can experience this heavenly kingdom in the sweet by and by. The good news is that the Kingdom of God can be experienced in the nasty here and now! Jesus came to earth as an ambassador of heaven to reveal to mankind the character and ability of God, and to invite mankind to participate in this Divine life. He came to show us what heavenly culture is all about.

Culture is defined as an integrated pattern of knowledge, beliefs, values and behavior that is learned, applied and passed down to succeeding generations. Basically, a culture is an environment that accepts or rejects people or ideas based on their compliance to its core values and beliefs. So when Jesus arrived on the scene, teaching the core values of heavenly culture and demonstrating various aspects of this culture by healing the sick and liberating the oppressed, the religious culture of the day naturally rejected the environment he produced everywhere he went. This is what is called "culture clash."

Once the cat was out of the bag, war was inevitable. The powers behind human culture began to adamantly oppose the Power behind heavenly culture. This was a knee-jerk reaction to the direct hit they took when Jesus opened up his mouth to contrast heaven's culture to the religious culture that dominated Israel at that time. Jesus did this with pinpoint accuracy in his famous Sermon on the Mount discourse by saying: *"Blessed are the poor in spirit, for theirs is the kingdom of heaven."* He then finished this list of Beatitudes by saying that *"those who are persecuted for righteousness sake are blessed because theirs is the kingdom of heaven"*

Jesus didn't say that the humble would go to heaven one day. And he didn't say that those who are persecuted would be blessed one day when they got to heaven. He said that the Kingdom of heaven presently belongs to those who are humble enough to receive it and bold enough to proclaim it in the midst of a culture that opposes it. In essence, Jesus said that the blessing the equivalent of accessing to resources of heaven in the earth. Only the humble can receive this new heavenly culture into their lives, and only the courageous can thrive in the midst of a culture that seeks to shape everything within its reach.

APOSTOLIC ORDER

-Every local church is a combination of heavenly culture and earthly culture. Apostles have a unique vantage point to make a distinction between heavenly culture and the parts of earthly culture that contradict the Kingdom of God. They also have a distinct ability to dismantle the thought processes that support that which is not built according to the pattern in heaven. Their God-given ability to set divine order out of chaos and dysfunction doesn't always make people feel good, but it prepares the church for forward movement instead of being stuck in yesterday.

ADOLESCENT PASTORS

Culture Clash   *Seeing the Invisible*

-Note to preachers: just because you have a platform and a pulpit doesn't mean you should preach what you want. Your latest and greatest revelation, although it may build your ego to preach it the first chance you get, might not build up the church if they need to hear something else first.

Remember that Jesus promised to build his church, not your ministry. So if you insist on building your ego by displaying your revelation at the expense of what people truly need, that shows that although you have the ability to get a girl pregnant, you're still not ready to be a mature father.

GIVING WITHOUT STRINGS

-If you truly walk in love, you will give with no strings attached. If you give with strings attached you are looking to man to reward you instead of God. However, if a relationship is one-sided, you need to make some adjustments to make things healthy. God has not called you to be a doormat either!

-Anything that seems to be spiritual but happens without the Holy Spirit's influence is actually religious.

-God loves to confound the wise through those who don't seem to measure up.

-Resisting the temptation to say what you want to say, when what is needed is altogether different, makes for peace. But not speaking up when it's time to say something is deceptively divisive. Don't sweep dirt under the rug. Eventually it will trip you up!!

VALIDATION

-The tendency to compare ourselves with others is usually rooted in insecurity. If we care more about what people think about us than what God thinks about us, it's easy to look for ways to validate our identity in our own mind and in the sight of others.

In that scenario, the weaknesses of others are leveraged to magnify your strengths. But at other times the strengths of others can be used to justify the magnification of your weaknesses. We shouldn't think too highly of ourselves, but we should also guard against walking in condemnation because we don't feel we measure up to the expectations of others due to our substandard performance.

"For those who walk after the Spirit there is no condemnation." That's because you take your cues from Him and not the opinions of others, or even your own opinion for that matter.

Be encouraged to look to God to validate you, to establish your identity. Set your focus on Him, what He is saying to you and what He is doing in your life. Let people think what they will. You don't have anything to prove. Your faith pleases God, not your efforts to please others.

PUTTING THE PIECES TOGETHER

Culture Clash   *Seeing the Invisible*

-What if **Acts 1:8** applied to every local church? *"...be witnesses to Me in Jerusalem, and in all Judea and Samaria, and to the end of the earth."*

What if we took seriously our role to represent Christ, not just within the four walls of our local church, but in our community, in our region and nation, and in the nations of the world? What if we reached out to give to and to receive from the rest of the body of Christ in our community, region and nation, and the nations of the world?

What if we placed great importance on what Jesus said in **Matthew 4:4** *"Man shall not live by bread alone, but by every word that proceeds from the mouth of the Father"*? What is God saying through the rest of the body that applies to you personally and to your local church? And vice versa, what is God saying to you that others need to hear?

Being a *"witness to Christ"* obviously doesn't mean we try to evangelize him! Lol. It means we lay our lives down for him like he laid down his life for us! Our lives point others to who he is and what he is saying to them. We do that by sacrificing our personal comfort for the sake of others, realizing we need the rest of his body and vice versa. We take seriously our privilege and responsibility of hearing his voice and making his voice known for others to hear. And we take seriously what he is saying to others that applies to us.

In **Colossians 4:16** Paul encourages the church in Colossae to exchange epistles with the church in Laodicea. Paul obviously believed that what God was speaking to both of these churches applied to others. Paul was encouraging a

Culture Clash *Seeing the Invisible*

regional relationship between churches to bring encouragement and mutual edification. What was a revelation to one could then become a revelation to the other. What was a strength for one could help strengthen the other.

Sometimes we get so focused on what God is saying directly to us that we forget that we only see in part! What other parts are we missing? What is God saying to others that applies to us? What is God saying to us that applies to others? We need to pursue relationships outside the local church for this very reason, especially leaders. A local church is not the body of Christ. It is a part of the body of Christ. No local church is complete in itself. We need one another, more than some would admit and more than most realize.

The benefit of receiving ministry from those not immersed in our local church culture is that they are sometimes enabled by the Lord to see things that are inconsistent with the Kingdom that have become normal to us. The opportunity then arises to learn new things, to make adjustments in our perspective and to be further conformed to the image of Christ.

May God supernaturally connect his body in this season just like **Ezekiel 37,** making it possible for us to receive every word from heaven that we need, strengthening and equipping us to fulfill our local assignment and for the church to arise across the earth to fulfill our commission to glorify His name!

-**Acts 1:7-8** *"...it is not for you to know times or seasons the Father has put in his own authority. But you shall receive power*

Culture Clash *Seeing the Invisible*

when the Holy Spirit has come upon you; and you shall be witnesses to me..."

It would be nice if people would stop spending their time trying to figure out what's going to happen, and start making something happen! You don't get rewarded for a perfect understanding of the "end times." You get rewarded for doing your part in the "end times!"

MEGA CHURCHES

-The closest thing we have to mega-churches in the NT are the churches in Jerusalem and Ephesus.

Jesus clearly told his disciples in **Acts 1:8** to be witnesses in Jerusalem, Judea, Samaria and the uttermost parts of the earth. But as the Jerusalem church quickly grew into the thousands, the mandate to expand God's Kingdom influence throughout the world was seemingly buried beneath the excitement and apparent success of what was happening in Jerusalem. There was a certain degree of comfort and convenience in staying with what was familiar in Jerusalem versus venturing into the unknown in other parts of the world.

That's why in God's sovereignty He allowed major persecution as recorded in **Acts 8:1**, which caused the entire church except the apostles to be scattered throughout the region, causing the church to finally obey their original assignment. That forced people to be activated in ministry and the apostles to once again press in to make "disciples of

Culture Clash *Seeing the Invisible*

Christ," as opposed to being comfortable in their apparent ministry success.

Think about it. The apostles had to start all over! What grew to be tens of thousands of people was shrunk to twelve in a single day! In that moment they had the opportunity and responsibility to build from scratch all over again, this time with the great commission in mind. It is uncertain whether the Jerusalem church ever reached its pre-Acts 8 size, but the command to spread the gospel throughout the world I'm sure was taken more seriously.

God is not against mega-churches. In fact, He loves when thousands are brought into the family of God. What He's against is mega-churches leveraging their resources to build their own empire instead of expanding God's Kingdom throughout the world. The success of a church is not measured solely by the number of people attending its services, but also by the number of believers who come into maturity and who are fulfilling their assignment, which includes planting other churches and spreading the gospel around the world.

The church of Ephesus also quickly grew to nearly 50,000 but the apostle Paul made sure it didn't repeat the mistake Jerusalem made. He established a Bible School there, training at least 7 of his spiritual sons for apostolic ministry, who then spread out throughout the region of Asia Minor to plant new churches. Ephesus leveraged their spiritual resources, not to build themselves up, but to obey the call of **Acts 1:8**, so much so that **Acts 19** says that all who dwelt in the region of Asia Minor heard the word of the Lord within 2 years!

Culture Clash   *Seeing the Invisible*

The truth is, quality always trumps quantity. Of course, God loves large quantities of people coming into relationship with Him. But he greatly desires for all of His children to come into maturity so they can do the works of their ministry and see the Kingdom of heaven spread throughout the earth.

When we value quantity over quality because of the apparent success of financial gain and notoriety, we fall victim to the Jerusalem trap, valuing our own comfort over the pain others experience in other regions. When we won't do our part to expand God's Kingdom throughout the world, we're doing what the Babylonians did in **Genesis 11**: making a name for ourselves instead of glorifying His name!!

-Much of what goes on in churches today is not initiated by the Spirit. It is emotion-driven, intellect-inspired or ambition-fueled. Jesus promised to build His church but if we insist on doing it our way, what are we really building? Possibly an Ishmael that appears to have God's blessing at times, but doesn't have His approval. Problem is, our Ishmaels are the very thing that hinder our Isaacs from fulfilling their purpose!

GOD IS SO COOL!

-God is so cool that you can make the biggest mistake in the world, and He will help you not only recover and get back on the right path, but He will redeem lost time and use your mistake to make you more like Him and more effective in ministering to others!!!!! Yes, He is that cool!!!!

Culture Clash   *Seeing the Invisible*

-What has God spoken to you that you have yet to respond to? There are blessings awaiting your obedience, but don't deceive yourself, because there are also consequences for dismissing the word of the Lord.

RESPONDING TO DISCERNMENT

-Just because you see something doesn't mean you should say something.

Sometimes God reveals things to you through your discernment to protect you. At other times to prepare you. But also so you can pray about certain things, giving God the faith He needs to intervene in a situation.

Giving voice to your discernment prematurely or to the wrong people without giving consideration for the above mentioned items can actually be counterproductive.

Before you say it, pray it. Ask God why He showed you what you saw and ask Him for wisdom to respond accordingly.

-What you choose to reveal or conceal in a relationship will determine the level of trust, intimacy and commitment. Don't withhold what someone has a right to know, but at the same time, don't disclose what someone hasn't earned the right to hear. Share what others can bear with you, not what they can't handle. Otherwise, it could backfire on you.

Culture Clash   *Seeing the Invisible*

FRAME YOUR WORLD WITH YOUR WORDS

-The Word in your mouth is capable of revolutionizing your life!

Release your faith through your words and watch your life come into alignment with your purpose! The Word is a sword that cuts off every attempt the devil makes to hinder your progress, and it is a tool to build your life according to God's design. Do yourself a favor, pull it out of its sheath and wield it with the authority God has given you!

-It's unfortunate when people don't receive what God has put in you for them because they can't see past your humanity. Or worse yet, because they want to use your God-given gift for their advantage.

YOUR WORDS ARE WEAPONS OF HIS CHOICE

-The devil strategizes how he can steal, kill and destroy your life and purpose. It's your responsibility to discern his schemes and overcome his plots by the word of God and the leading of the Spirit. Here's a few things to be aware of:

- -He deceives perspective with lies
- -He delays progress with religion
- -He defiles purity with carnality
- -He distracts passion with unhealthy relationships
- -He dilutes power with fear

Culture Clash   *Seeing the Invisible*

But *"Greater is He that is in you than he that is in the world." "No weapon formed against you will prosper. Every tongue that rises up against <u>you will condemn</u>!"* Did you get that? It's your responsibility to condemn, or render ineffective, every tongue that rises up against you. That's why it's crucial to maintain a close relationship with the Lord and those He assigns for your life. Without those two things, you aren't equipped with the armor of God to stand against the wiles or schemes of the devil.

Jesus came that you may have life that becomes more abundant every day! Follow His voice and the enemy will be exposed by the light. And your path will be brighter and brighter!!

-When you're traveling down what seems to be a dead-end street, don't forget that what may feel like a tomb can actually be a womb where God births greatness in you! God is an expert at turning things around!!

TOO MUCH OF A GOOD THING

-One of the failures of many apostolic and prophetic churches today is the undervaluing of the pastoral, evangelistic and teaching gifts.

1. Without an evangelistic thrust, how do you expect to win the lost?

2. Without pastoral grace, how do you expect to adequately care for believers?

3. Without a teaching flow, how do you expect people to be grounded in foundational truth?

No wonder most apostolic and prophetic churches don't seem to grow very large. If they're not winning the lost or caring for those who are saved or grounding people in foundational truth, and are yet challenging people to continuously change, don't you think discouragement could set in?

Too much correction and rebuke in proportion to encouragement and comfort can be counterproductive! That's great that you don't compromise the truth in order to get more butts in seats and dollars in the offering. But please, let's aim to have the fullness of Christ in our midst, not just your favorite two gifts. It's possible to have too much of a good thing when that comes at the expense of not having enough of other things you need as well!

GOD KNOWS WHAT HE'S DOING

-The next time you can't figure out what's going on in your life, remember the last time God proved that His ways are higher than your ways! Sometimes you just gotta' trust that He knows what He's doing, especially when you don't understand. It will make sense later. Keep walking!!

Culture Clash   *Seeing the Invisible*

It's not called a walk of faith for no reason! If you understood everything you wouldn't need faith. Just listen and obey, there's no other way, than to trust in Jesus!!

-The love of money is quite possibly the biggest hindrance to the American church adequately representing the Kingdom of God. As long as we are controlled by the world system we will not have the ability to transform the world around us.

-When truth emerges to challenge the status quo of religious indoctrination, truth quickly gets dismissed and the character of those who proclaim it gets maligned. All in the name of defending what some presume to be the truth, when in fact what they are trying to protect are personal opinions and doctrines of men. And the stronger the resistance to the truth, the more likely a doctrine of devils is getting uprooted.

BEFORE YOU LEAVE YOUR CHURCH

-Wondering whether you are in the right church or not? Here's some factors to consider if that is the case:

1. Are you confident that the Lord led you there?
2. How have you grown since you have been there?
3. How have your gifts been utilized there?
4. What relationships have developed since you've been there?
5. Does your leadership sincerely care for you?

Culture Clash *Seeing the Invisible*

6. Is your church progressively manifesting the Kingdom of God?

7. Is the vision of the house large enough to include what God has put into your heart to do?

8. Does your church welcome all 5-fold ministries and all 9 gifts of the Spirit?

9. Does your church resemble a family or does it seem to function more like a business?

10. Is your leadership abusive and/or dealing with serious moral failure?

11. Is there offense in your heart that is undealt with?

12. Are there spiritual nutrients you are craving that are absent from your church's DNA?

13. Is rebellion manifesting in your heart because you have refused correction?

14. Is your flesh leading you to find a more relaxed church environment that doesn't challenge you to get involved, take action, repent or give?

15. Is the grass really greener on the other side?

16. Have you really prayed about this decision or are you responding to your emotions?

17. Is team ministry established in the culture of your church, or is it a one-man show?

18. Have you been attending your church out of convenience (close to your house, family or friends attend there, your childhood church, etc.)

19. Are you attending church because of ministry opportunities only?

20. If you were not paid would you still attend your church?

Culture Clash   *Seeing the Invisible*

Please follow the Lord's leading in line with the Word of God. Don't remained trapped by tradition or driven by your flesh. And certainly don't tolerate abuse. My prayer is that this list, which is by no means all-inclusive, can help you face some questions you may not have considered in the process of determining if you need to change churches, and if so, where to go from here.

One thing's for sure, God has a place for you. Don't throw in the towel without first working through the issues of your heart, reconciling with people who may have hurt you and praying things through. And by all means, talk with your pastor. Otherwise, you will carry baggage to the next place and start this process all over again. God wants you to be planted, but sometimes it is necessary to uproot yourself for your own spiritual growth and the fulfillment of your calling. But please don't pull the trigger until you've patiently waited on the Lord to make things clear to you.

-Peace is priceless, especially after emerging from the fight of your life! Knowing the battle is over and seeing God put the pieces of your life back together again gives you the peace of mind to know your future is brighter than your past! Then beginning to walk into a new season with grace to handle challenges differently than before gives you confidence that as long as you focus on what God is saying, everything will work out in your favor!

TRANSFERRING GRACE

-All grace originates with God but it can be transferred from one person to another, making what is easy for the giver easier for the recipient.

This is what is meant by **Ephesians 4**. We all receive grace from God (:7) but we also need to receive grace from each other (:12) in order to be fully equipped for our assignment and to become mature in Christ.

-The wrong kind of compromise is a result of responding to the fear that God will not come through for you. The right kind of compromise is a result of humbly acknowledging that you don't have all the answers.

DEFINING RELATIONSHIPS

-It is critical that you allow God to define relationships for you: the purpose and season of each relationship. Don't force a relationship into a preconceived mold of what you think it should be. Let the Father do what He does best: *"arranging the members in the body as pleases Him."*

-The fact that half the church doesn't show up when the senior leader is not present reveals that that particular local church is not Christ-centered, it is personality-driven and gift-focused. We need churches that are built on the revelation of Who He is, not who we are! (**Mt 16:18-19**)

EQUIP THE SAINTS

Culture Clash   *Seeing the Invisible*

-A grassroots movement of the Spirit has already begun, activating saints to do supernatural ministry for the glory of God. But just because God is with you performing signs and wonders doesn't mean you no longer need leadership! Just because you've been empowered and are releasing that power to others doesn't mean you no longer have a need to be further-equipped!

Read **Acts 11**. It tells the story of how the church at Antioch was birthed through ordinary disciples with extraordinary power. But once the leadership at the church at Jerusalem heard about it, they sent Barnabas to see what was going on. He recognized the grace of God in action, saints doing the works of the ministry, and encouraged them to continue in that flow. But from that point on, Barnabas and Paul came to bring strength, order and further equipping of the church there.

As a result of leadership taking their place in the lives of ministering saints, the ministry became even more effective and other leaders began to emerge. Because Paul and Barnabas built the church on the foundation of Christ, not keeping people dependent on themselves, they were sent on their missionary journey only one year later, and the church at Antioch continued to move forward without them!

May God's grace continue to equip all of God's people for the work of the ministry, but don't forget the importance of leadership in the family of God. We will always need it, no matter how mature and strong we become. And may God's leadership empower all of God's people for ministry, building their dependency on the Spirit and not themselves.

Culture Clash   *Seeing the Invisible*

BAKING BRICKS FOR PHARAOH

-It saddens my heart when pastors are more excited about their members being faithful attendees and givers than actually maturing in Christ and fulfilling their calling. Last time I checked, parents are there to raise up children to maturity so they can have their own families.

Without this family perspective of church, we tend to gravitate toward the business/political model of church where people exist to serve the vision of the house. Yes, there is one vision of the house, but it is not to extend the kingdom of the CEO senior pastor at the top, it is to extend the Kingdom of God and to build His church, which is made up of God's sons and daughters.

Without a true Kingdom perspective, people eventually feel like they're baking bricks for Pharaoh. In that scenario, they are keeping the machine running by their presence, pocketbook and volunteer service. This was never God's intention for His family.

-Dare to believe God in the face of contrary evidence!

SOWING & REAPING

-Sowing and reaping is much more than financial. It is a spiritual principle that manifests in the financial realm, but also in every other aspect of life. According to **Galatians 6**, it is about *"sowing to the Spirit"* when you are given the opportunity to do so. This I believe, is about responding to the Spirit's leading to give of your time, talent and/or treasure to people you are in relationship with or who you receive ministry from, to bless their life and further the Kingdom of God.

The same passage says *"if we sow to the Spirit, we will reap of the Spirit everlasting life."* I believe that everlasting life is not heaven per se, but every Kingdom resource in heaven that we need to move forward on our journey to fulfill divine purpose. Ultimately, our reaping comes from the Spirit, not people. But our reaping manifests in money at times and God uses people to get it to us. But our source is our Father, not the people we sow into. God causes this spiritual cycle to bless us as we are a blessing to others.

SUCCESS OF THE CHURCH

-The true success of a church is not measured by the amount of butts in seats or dollars in offering plates, especially when the truth has been diluted to increase those numbers. True success is measured by the tangible presence of Jesus when we gather in His name, by the depth His truth penetrates and transforms our hearts, and by the dimension His Kingdom expands through our lives in the region surrounding our gatherings. Not everything is as it seems!

-We don't need a massage to make us feel good, we need a message that provokes us to become more like Christ and to love people aggressively! We need to prioritize the needs of others above our wants.

QUALIFICATIONS OF LEADERS

-If we actually used **I Timothy 3** and **Titus 2** as guidelines for putting people into ministry, as opposed to gifts and talents, we would have less illegitimate churches led by immature or misplaced leaders, not to mention we wouldn't see so many leaders fall into gross sin. If these guidelines were good enough for the first century church, they apply to us today.

-If you spend more time with your spiritual sons and daughters than your natural children, something may be wrong. Please don't sacrifice your children on the altar of your ministry.

-If you are driven by selfish ambition to be successful in ministry in the eyes of man, your marriage will suffer. But if you determine to live and minister by grace, your marriage will flourish and God will see that your ministry will flourish as well.

-Discernment is dulled by your desires to the degree that your desires aren't submitted to His will. You deceive yourself when you ask God to bless what you want. Perhaps you

Culture Clash   *Seeing the Invisible*

should discover what God wants first, then ask God to bless that!

YOU CAN DO IT!

-There's no CAN'T in the Kingdom! If you have a Word on it, go after it! It's yours for the taking! You CAN do all things through Christ!"

The apostle Paul said that *"we must through many tribulations enter the Kingdom of God!"* With every promise from God comes distractions to take your attention off the One who promised and onto contrary circumstances. After receiving a Kingdom revelation, you must embrace a "Can Do mentality," realizing you have an inheritance that must be accessed in order for your God-given dreams to be fulfilled.

Only those who focus on their own resources say "I can't." When you know you are a child of the King and therefore have an unlimited supply to draw from, you will say with Paul," *I can do all things through Christ who strengthens me!*"

Your mountain may seem insurmountable but keep in mind, your mountain knows your voice. Speak those things that aren't as though they are and they shall be!! You CAN do it!!

-If we could see what's hindering our forward progress, we would be more receptive to the ministry of the Holy Spirit to lead us into all truth, which includes leading us out of partial truths and outright lies. But we often resist the prompting of the Spirit to move forward because we don't see our current beliefs and traditions as being the very problem.

-Azusa was not just the birth of a revival, it was also a reformation. It reformed theology. It reformed traditions and church structures. It reformed lifestyles. Today we must welcome the spirit of reformation if we are to sustain revival!

DETOXIFICATION

-God told Joshua that if they did not drive out all the nations from their Promised Land, that those nations would eventually become thorns in their sides and pricks in their eyes. By doing so, instead of expanding God's Kingdom rule to the new world around them, they would be changed by their surrounding culture.

It was for this same reason that God told them not to marry into the other nations. God wasn't against interracial marriages, He was against false religions and earthly value systems infiltrating His people's lives and hindering their progress.

Today, the world has contaminated much of the church, hindering our ability to change the world around us, extending His kingdom rule. What we need more than revival is reformation, internal change to detoxify us of the world's influence so we will have the authority to represent God well in the earth. If we only seek new wine and assume our wineskin needs no alteration, we won't have the sustained results God has in mind, which is to transform the world around us.

-When pretty programs replace the power of God in churches today, there no longer is an atmosphere that is conducive for miracles and deliverance when people need it the most.

-There are windows of opportunity that need to be discerned and accessed quickly because they will close as quickly as they open. Sometimes you just have to strike while the iron is hot!! Timing is crucial!

CHURCH HURT

-There are tens of thousands of believers who no longer attend church because of church hurt. There are at least that many believers who attend church but are somewhat distant, not involved in ministry in any way and certainly not engaged in personal relationships outside of church services. If healthy believers would take seriously their role as peacemakers, and restore their brothers and sisters who are hurting, the body of Christ would edify itself and an army of soul winners would assemble to revolutionize regions for God's Kingdom!

TWO KINDS OF SIGNS

-Mark 16:15-20

Culture Clash   *Seeing the Invisible*

There are actually two different kinds of signs in this text. Signs that follow those who believe the Word in **verse 17** and accompanying signs that confirm the Word that is preached in **verse 20**. Signs that follow people and signs that confirm the Word. I know you may have thought they are one and the same but consider this:

We tend to focus on the external signs listed in this passage: casting out demons, healing the sick and speaking in tongues, but neglect the internal signs (evidence) that the Word is taking effect in people's hearts.

Isaiah prophesied that God's people would be *"for signs and wonders"* to the people around them. Paul said that we are to become *"living epistles, written by the Holy Spirit and read of all men."*

In other words, God wants there to be no distance between the Word we believe and preach and the Word that we live. We need to be one with the Word. Our lives need to become signs (indications) that the Word is alive. This happens by the transformation of the Holy Spirit through the renewing of our minds.

I think the charismatic church has for the most part undervalued the internal signs that the Holy Spirit is at work because it has valued gifts more than character.

Consider **Matthew 7:15-27**, specifically **verses 22-23**: *"Many will say to me in that day, Lord, Lord have we not prophesied in your name, cast out demons in your name and done many wonders (signs) in your name? And I will declare to them, I never knew you; depart from me, you who practice*

Culture Clash *Seeing the Invisible*

lawlessness!" They identified in word only, using the authority of Jesus' name to perform signs and wonders, but did not allow His name (identity) to change who they were through personal relationship. Signs confirmed the validity of the Word but not the legitimacy of their relationship with Christ.

If there's anything we need to learn from this passage, it is to value internal character more than external gifts in operation. It's possible for God to honor His Word with signs and wonders, even when the one preaching the Word isn't actively living the Word. But don't be deceived, this doesn't mean those signs validate the people preaching the Word out of their mouths, especially when their hearts and lives aren't one with the Word.

Jesus said to know people by their fruit, evidence that they have an intimate relationship with Christ that is conforming their character to Christ, not by their gifts. That means we can recognize false prophets by examining if they are one with the Word, if they show evidence of godly character, not by how many signs and wonders are displayed in their meetings.

Consider the church in Corinth. Although they "*came behind in no gift and the testimony of Christ was confirmed in them*" through signs and wonders, there was little internal evidence (signs) that the Word was taking effect within. The reason why **I and II Corinthians** were so long is because of all the sin Paul had to address. They weren't even close to being one with the Word! Division, strife, envy, jealousy, insecurity, carnal comparisons and competition, lawsuits, drunkenness and sexual immorality to name a few issues!

Culture Clash   *Seeing the Invisible*

But herein lies the grace of God. God places His gifts in imperfect vessels and as we continue to receive His Word into our lives, we are perfected along the way. God confirms His Word with signs and wonders, and as we continue in our pursuit to know Christ more, we become signs and wonders. Concrete evidence that we have been with Jesus becomes visible for all to see.

Here's a few internal signs that confirm that the Word is taking effect in our hearts and lives:

1. False doctrine, philosophy and traditions of men rooted out
2. Kingdom truth and understanding established in place of old paradigms
3. Motives and attitudes of the heart purified
4. God's will for your life revealed
5. Wisdom granted to guide daily decisions
6. Godly character developed and exemplified through daily life and relationships
7. Consistent decisions that are in line with the calling of God

Many people also make the false assumption that supernatural manifestations after the Word is preached validates the truthfulness of the Word they just heard. Spiritual gifts don't confirm false doctrine any more than they justify sinful lifestyles. It's possible to be off in our theology and for spiritual gifts to still be in operation. After all, God doesn't wait until we are perfect before He uses us. He perfects us along the way.

Culture Clash *Seeing the Invisible*

I pray that God shifts our focus from what appears <u>spectacular</u> to what is truly <u>supernatural.</u> I believe we can have the best of both worlds: fruit and gifts, but knowing Jesus has to be our focus, not striving to establish our own identity by using God's gifts to exalt ourselves!

-Birds of a feather may flock together, but wise people realize the importance of diversity, accessing grace in people who are different than you. In God's Kingdom, a unified diversity accelerates your spiritual growth and protects you from stagnation.

-The spirit of reformation at work <u>in you</u> will sustain the spirit of revival flowing <u>through you</u>. It can and should be a way of life! As the word declares, *"we should walk in newness of life."*

FIVE-FOLD GRACE

-Contrary to popular belief, pastors are not supposed to do the works of the ministry. They are called by God to equip the saints to do the works of the ministry, according to **Ephesians 4:11-12**. In fact, all of the five-fold ministry gifts mentioned in this verse are assigned to teach and train the saints to do what is easy for them to do.

They are positioned to impart grace to the rest of the body, which equips us to be fruitful in our assignments. Without an equipping from all five-fold graces, we are ill-equipped to fulfill our callings and do not have the whole armor protecting us from the devil's schemes, which hinder us in our assignments.

And this goes for all five-fold ministers as well! Just because you are gifted with a five-fold leadership capacity does not mean you are exempt from these things. In order to be mature, in order to be properly equipped and adequately protected, we all need these graces in our lives!!

That's because we all need the fullness of Christ to be balanced and seasoned in the things of God. May God deliver us from our preferences and from traditions that keep us ill-equipped to fulfill our callings! A huge element that is often neglected in the discussion of spiritual covering is a well-balanced spiritual diet of five-fold grace via ministry we receive and relationships we engage in.

Attending a church, putting an offering in the bucket and calling someone your pastor doesn't impress the devil. He still deceives, distracts and destroys millions of believers in this category. What the devil is afraid of is when believers access the fullness of Christ through five-fold grace that thoroughly equips them to overcome every spiritual attack on their way to fulfill God-given vision!

APOSTOLIC MUSIC

-We've grown accustomed to prophetic music over the last 30 years that creates an atmosphere to hear and see in the spirit, as well as to release through the power of words the intention and insight of God. We are about to experience a new phenomenon in the body of Christ for all who will receive it: <u>apostolic music</u> that creates a culture of glory in the atmosphere, bringing the intention of God into reality.

Miracles and deliverance, supernatural manifestations, breakthrough revelation, accelerated answered prayers and unprecedented unified relationships will be the byproducts of this new apostolic flow. It's about to be released through minstrels who know how to tap into an apostolic vein that releases into the natural realm what has been stored up in the spirit. Wow!! I want some of that!

NEW WINE SKINS

-Why is it that we tend to believe God for new wine far more than we believe God for a new wineskin? Perhaps that is evidence that our flesh is more involved in our prayer lives than our spirit. We love for God to bless us, but our fleshly nature resists Him changing us. Lord, transform our wineskins so the wine from heaven will not be wasted on our fleshly appetites to receive the glory that only belongs to You!

THE POWER OF A REMINDER

-When I started ministering the Word, I aimed to reveal my latest and greatest revelations to the world in an attempt to prove my spirituality and to gain respect from others. Then I realized how clearly I showed the world my immaturity. Peter encouraged spiritual elders to remind people of what they had already been taught.

The purpose of a reminder is not just to rekindle information that was previously heard. It is to strengthen the depth of one's understanding of truth and to encourage application of what has been learned. It can also empower people with the ability to use that truth to minister to others.

What good does a powerful revelation do if people don't have a firm enough grip on it to understand, apply and minister it to others? Are we looking for the "ooh's and ah's" of spiritual fireworks or are we aiming to transform a generation with the power of God's Word?

FULFILLING PROPHETIC WORDS

-Some prophetic words require your participation for fulfillment. Exercising your faith by confessing, praying and declaring what God has said is a good place to start. Then believing God for wisdom so your life is in sync with that word is in order. Finally, taking steps of faith in response to wisdom revealed will position you to receive in manifestation what has been conceived in your spirit.

If you still lack fulfillment at this point, go back to step one. But keep in mind, some words also have timing attached to them. In other words, God won't release their fulfillment until you are mature enough to handle it. There may be other factors involved such as the participation of other people, unresolved issues in your heart or demonic hindrance, but rest assured, if God said it He can and will do it!

But He often wants your cooperation in the process to develop your faith muscles. As Peter said, *"we are partakers of the divine nature."* God creates with His Word and we are part of this process. Don't give up on your Word, fully agree with it in the face of contrary evidence!

-When the power of love is truly celebrated more than spiritual gifts, the church will experience an inner transformation that will make revival a way of life instead of an occasional event.

-Spiritual momentum is initiated by your response to spiritual manifestations. No response is dangerous because it minimizes the ministry of the Holy Spirit and opens the door to the enemy of your soul.

THE REFORMERS ARE COMING

-Here's what I heard while praying recently: "There's a whole generation of reformers God is raising up in this hour. Not just those who will simply improve our thinking and way of life, but those who will introduce major paradigm shifts, causing us to re-evaluate our beliefs, practices and priorities.

Don't resist them or the words that come out of their mouths, because by doing so you will be rejecting the Lord who raised them up and the One who is speaking through them. Yes, you need to test the spirits. But be careful not to pre-judge what is released because you don't approve of the package. Don't judge a book by its cover. Prepare your hearts for change, for change is coming." Does anyone have an ear to hear?

Culture Clash   *Seeing the Invisible*

-When your actions speak louder than your words, the hypocrisy of your heart is on display for all to see. You need to be synchronized by the power of the Word, integrated by the inner working of the Spirit.

CHARIS-MANIACS

-The charismatic church desperately needs to be delivered from what appears spectacular so it can access what is truly supernatural. Not everything is what it appears to be!

-If staring at the back of someone's head for two hours every Sunday morning is your idea of fellowship, you might need a new revelation of what church is all about!

-No matter what you say, somebody will disagree with it. No matter what you do, somebody won't like it. I say live to please the One who died for you and let the chips fall where they may!

TRUE SPIRITUALITY

-It's easy to assume you're spiritual based on dreams, visions, prophecies and spiritual gifts, but those supernatural things don't prove you're spirituality. They give us an opportunity to align with our Kingdom purpose. It's the fruit of the Spirit and the ability to tame our flesh that reveal our true spirituality, which simply means living from your spirit.

The Corinthians *"came behind in no spiritual gift,"* or in other words, they were the elite in spiritual gifts, and yet Paul addressed them as babes in Christ! The books of **I and II Corinthians** were the longest of Paul's epistles next to Romans because of all the junk in their lives he had to put in order: division, envy, drunkenness, sexual sin, suing one another, etc. He didn't forbid spiritual gifts, he just encouraged them to value character over gifting. And so should we!!

CODEPENDENCE

-Jesus told his disciples and the multitudes not to be called 'rabbi' or 'teacher' nor to call anyone 'father.' This can easily be taken out of context if you don't use your brain or read the rest of the scriptures.

Obviously it's normal to refer to your biological father as 'father' and the apostle Paul referred to himself as a spiritual father. So there must be a deeper meaning. Also, although this passage says there's only one Teacher, scripture makes it clear that God gave the church teachers within the framework of the five-fold ministry. So once again, there's something beneath the surface Jesus was trying to bring to their and our attention.

Jesus was making reference to the Pharisees and the relationship the people had to the Pharisees. Jesus was redefining leadership roles within the New Covenant of grace. His command was for people to not allow religious leaders to take God's place in their life in any way. God is our Father and it's not the role of leadership to get in the way, but to help us in our relationship with Him. So we need to guard our hearts so we don't give glory to men that only God deserves.

On the flip side, Jesus commanded his disciples, the core group of leaders being trained to administer the New Covenant of grace, to be careful in leading people in such a way so as to not get in the way of their relationship with the Father.

Previous to this transitional season, people had to depend on leadership to reveal God to them, and unfortunately this got to the heads of many leaders. Then pride caused them to elevate themselves above their rightful place. So Jesus was bringing order to this issue as well as showing us that things were to be different in the New Covenant.

In the OT, only a select few at special times heard God speak and had the anointing come upon them. Now we all hear God speak and have the anointing within. Codependency now must bow the knee to interdependence. We still need leaders to guide us, but we shouldn't be overly dependent upon them when the Spirit of God lives inside us.

TRUE HONOR

-*"Give honor to whom honor is due."*

"Whatever you do in word or deed, do it as unto the Lord."

When someone is attempting to "honor me" by serving or giving in whatever capacity, I can sometimes feel that something is not right. Sometimes I feel that people are

Culture Clash   *Seeing the Invisible*

carrying out a particular tradition more than they are truly honoring the gift of God in me.

At other times, I feel that people are going beyond "honor" into a mode of idolatry, like I'm somebody important and they get to rub elbows with me. And then there are those who seem to be engaging in religious politics. They think that if they serve me, then I owe them some kind of reward.

But true honor is rooted in love and respect. A love for God, His Word and the gifts God has put in all of us, not just those who have a microphone in their hand. Respect comes from an awareness that God has brought someone into your life to minister to you, whether in public ministry or personal relationship. So you honor them by positioning yourself to receive from their gift, not allowing their humanity to hinder your receptivity. Because of respect, their words have more weight in your heart than those you are not in relationship with.

True honor is not doing for me what I am perfectly capable of doing myself. It is a servant-like attitude that looks for ways to serve when necessary that can make it easier for one to minister and for others to receive.

If the truth were told, honor goes both ways. We don't hear much about this because many who are in leadership roles in the body of Christ have been elevated at times above their rightful place, allowing idolatrous versions of honor to continue and for traditions to be carried out, which only obscure what true honor is.

Culture Clash *Seeing the Invisible*

The apostle Paul refused to be idolized, tearing his cloak in disgust when people wanted to sacrifice to him. The apostle Peter told people *"why do you look at us as if we made this man whole?!"* He refused to receive glory that only belonged to the Lord.

"Honor one another."

Leadership today has a responsibility to refuse idolatry, to break free from traditions of men and to avoid the childish games of religious politics. But we need to take it a step further. We need to honor those we serve. It goes both ways. We need to respect everyone we minister to because they belong to God, not us. Although we may consider some to be our "spiritual children" they are first and foremost children of God!

We don't own anyone! We are managers of the gifts God has given us and we are under-shepherds. Jesus is the Shepherd of their soul. We need to embrace our responsibility to serve others, honoring the gifts God has deposited within them, never taking advantage of them for our profit, but empowering them to be everything God created them to be.

May God establish the culture of honor in the church once again! Not a cheap, distorted version. But the true thing. We honor God by honoring one another. As Jesus told his disciples when sending them out to minister, *"If they receive you they receive me, and if they reject you they reject me."* Also, *"Whatsoever you do to the least of these, you do unto me."*

TOXIC RELATIONSHIPS

Culture Clash *Seeing the Invisible*

-Scripture encourages us to "*live at peace with all men, if at all possible.*" But there are times when it's not possible, when it's dangerous to our psyche, spiritual life and calling to remain in relationships with those who use and abuse us. For some, their very life can be in danger. In those cases, you must run for cover because the enemy is injecting spiritual poison into your bloodstream.

After you exit toxic relationships there is a season of detox, a season where the impurities that contaminated the flow of God's Spirit must be flushed out of your system. But it all starts with obeying the prompting of the Spirit to cut ungodly soul ties that are binding you to your past, instead of launching you into your destiny.

Faith must also be exercised for godly relationships to come into your life that will bring healing, deliverance and a fresh dose of heaven when you need it most. That way, you can get your past behind you and have a network of healthy relationships to protect you from this happening again.

Isolation is the strategy of the enemy to control you, which inevitably opens the door for the pure flow of God's Spirit in you to be diluted in power and polluted in purity. There is hope for you to recover and wisdom for you to be protected. But you need to press in your spirit for your own freedom. It won't come easily, but if you want to be free the Son will set you free indeed!

I Cor. 6:14 "*Do not be unequally yoked together...*"
I Cor. 6:17 "*Come out from among them... And I will receive you.*"

Culture Clash *Seeing the Invisible*

I Cor. 7:1 *"Therefore, having these promises beloved, let us cleanse ourselves from all filthiness of the flesh and spirit, perfecting holiness in the fear of God."*

-The antidote for resistance is persistence. Just make sure your persistence is connected to the leading of the Spirit to breakthrough obstacles on the way to your Kingdom assignment. I say this because there are times when God actually will resist your religious pride, which can be easily misinterpreted as the enemy. No, it's God keeping you from making a bigger mess of things! In this case, you just need to give up. Surrender to God because you're fighting an uphill battle! Humble yourself before Him, and then and only then, He will give you the grace you need for your assignment.

PREACHING A CUSTOM-FIT WORD

-For those who minister the Word on any level, I want to share something that may help you.

Before I minister to a church or gathering of leaders, I ask the Lord to make me sensitive to minister the most relevant message that is alive in me that will meet the deepest need of the people receiving the Word. Of course, God may give me something fresh that I haven't ministered before too.

I ask the Lord to make me aware of the overall maturity level of the people I will be ministering to, which becomes apparent as I begin speaking and gauge the reception and response to the Word. I don't want to feed a baby steak, nor do I want to give an adult a bottle of warm milk!

Culture Clash *Seeing the Invisible*

I also try to discern the revelation God has already established in their lives before I minister what I feel God is saying. And I discern where God is taking them. That way, I can custom fit the message God has already spoken to me to the people I'm speaking to. It will have a much greater impact than if I just preached it the way I received it.

These are prophetic/apostolic functions that can enhance our messages to better fit the lives of those we minister to. Seeing the big picture helps us with the details of the particular Word we deliver. And the more impartation of prophetic and apostolic anointing you receive, the more accurate you will be in the delivery of the Word.

Simply put, I discern the greatest need or lack in the people I will minister to as well as the most appropriate Word God has given me to minister to that need.

As the apostle Paul said in **Romans 1:11,** *"I long to see you, that I may impart to you some spiritual gift, so that you may be established."* And in **I Thess. 3:10,** *"night and day praying exceedingly that we may see your face and perfect what is lacking in your faith."*

It's one thing to bring forth a good Word. It's another thing to hit the bullseye with the God-Word, the right word at the right time at the appropriate level of maturity.

Let's ask God to increase our effectiveness in ministering what is on His heart for His people. Lord, make us more sensitive to what You are speaking to Your people so they can move forward in their journey toward their Kingdom assignment!

Culture Clash *Seeing the Invisible*

-Some apostles use their gift as a tool to build their kingdom and as a weapon to tear others down. It's time for a new generation of apostles to use their gift as an instrument of worship to glorify His name!!

-Don't sweat it when one door closes in your life. Another door will open that will explain why the first door needed to close. Sometimes our plans get trumped by God's plan! His ways are higher!

-When we have true spiritual contentment, there's nothing the devil can do to disrupt our peace. But if we're not careful we can develop a soulish contentment that keeps us from pressing into the Kingdom, losing our willingness to fight for what is ours.

RELIGIOUS MENTALITIES

-Religious people focus on what they HAVE TO do to measure up. Kingdom-minded people focus on what they CAN DO for the influence of heaven to increase in and through their lives.

Culture Clash   *Seeing the Invisible*

-Religion causes us to divide from one another in an attempt to dominate one another.

-Religion causes people to tolerate what they should dominate, causing people to be dominated by what they tolerate.

-Religion sometimes causes people to settle for less than what Jesus died for.

PRESSING INTO THE KINGDOM

-Unless we put forth concerted effort to go against the flow of the world system, which includes both religion and carnality, we will be swept up in the 'current' current. Yes, I meant to say that! Read it again to understand. Culture evolves into the image of the dominant powers that be. We the church can change the culture but we need to Press into the Kingdom to have the authority to do so.

-Substance matters. When you value the external presentation more than the internal reality you've been blinded to what really matters! Paul's sermons weren't pretty but his ministry was powerful! No amount of polished rhetoric can mask motives and attitudes that are bent on selfish living. Give me power first, then let me perfect the craft. Never the other way around. Let's not get the cart in

Culture Clash   *Seeing the Invisible*

front of the horse. Otherwise, your horse will not be happy! Lol

-The main weakness I see with our version of "the local church" is that it doesn't include all believers in each locality like it did in the first century. Nor does it include a unified leadership team in each locality. I'm afraid we're trying to run what is meant to be an 8 cylinder engine, on 4 cylinders! Change is on the horizon!

RETHINKING OFFERINGS

-This will get me in trouble with some preachers but frankly I don't care anymore. It amazes me how easily some preachers dismiss scripture when it doesn't work for their advantage. For example, when it comes to giving offerings we are clearly told in the Word that...

"Giving is accepted according to what one has"   -Give based on your personal budget.

"Give willingly"   -Make giving decisions based on your personal desires.

"I don't want you to be burdened with giving"   -Don't give too much if it is burdensome.

"Don't give grudgingly"   -Don't give with reservations or regrets.

"Don't give based on compulsion"   -Don't give under pressure or manipulation.

Culture Clash *Seeing the Invisible*

"*Give as you purpose in your heart*" -Give intentionally from rational thinking, not from external factors.

...and yet, it is a common practice for many charismatic preachers to raise the bar above the budgets of many saints, (not according to what they have) convincing them to give a specific dollar amount (that many really don't want to give) to stretch their faith in an emotionally-charged environment (compulsion) with the pressure of other people watching (manipulation), many times with a "God told me to tell you" attached to it (false prophecy) and a special prayer or prophecy for those who measure up to the $1000 offering (favoritism) or whatever creative amount they, I mean God, came up with, usually accompanied by a false promise of hope (1000 fold return) if people comply with the specific dollar amount offering (bribe).

Many believers jump on board, given the powerful revelation that is masterfully woven with the carnal offering, which is often taken at the high spiritual point of a service, either at the end of the message or immediately following a powerful flow of the Spirit, so as to legitimize the soulish appeal for money by what is truly spiritual.

Based on this method of raising offerings, anything less than what you're told to give is unacceptable, what you want to give is irrelevant, your budget doesn't matter, your financial burdens are of no concern to the preacher taking up the offering and you may end up regretting giving to your own financial detriment. And apparently manipulation, false prophecy, favoritism and bribery are temporarily exempted

Culture Clash   *Seeing the Invisible*

from the sin list, and you are not expected to think for yourself because it will be done for you!

I realize I'm putting a magnifying glass on an extreme example, but I think you get my point. There are extremes to everything including giving. And there are varying degrees of manipulation that are out of line with the Scriptures regarding giving, on both ends of the spectrum. I could paint a descriptive picture of a religious, poverty-minded offering too. They're equally as harmful.

Honestly, there's a time and place for leaders to encourage people to give sacrificially. Leaders are responsible to preach the whole counsel of God, which includes giving. But when leaders begin to push the envelope because of how it benefits them personally without regard to how it may affect others, that's when things get off. God never intended prosperity to come to preachers at the expense of the rest of God's people. God wants to bless us all.

Truthfully, Scripture encourages generosity and sacrificial giving at times, but it does not condone carnal methods to provoke believers to give. Giving should flow from a heart of love and should be guided by the faith that God will bring increase when we are led by the Spirit, not driven by the demands of men.

Believers sold land and houses in the first century church at Jerusalem, not because they were manipulated into doing so by the apostles, but because they were moved by the Spirit to love in tangible ways. But the proceeds didn't line the pockets of the apostles. Out of thousands of believers, not a

Culture Clash   *Seeing the Invisible*

single person lacked anything! It was the equivalent of a reverse offering. The people laid the money at the apostles' feet and finances were distributed to meet the needs of the community of believers.

Scripture does not say a select few were multi-millionaires while the vast majority barely got by. There was equality, families helping each other out, not a few big shots capitalizing on the generosity of the saints. Scripture warns of false prophets and false teachers taking advantage of believers for monetary gain, making merchandise of people. And yet today this practice goes on without being questioned. Perhaps we should read our Bibles more than we hear what others have to say.

The Word says to *"believe not every spirit"* and to *"test the spirits"* to see if they are of God. The best way to test people is with the Holy Textbook and the best way to know people is by their fruit. Problem is, false prophets tend to hide their private lives from the vast majority of the public. So walk in discernment and when push comes to shove, align yourself with what Peter came to the conclusion of: *"we ought to obey God rather than man."*

MANIPULATORS VS. MOTIVATORS

-Ok, here's the other side of the coin pertaining to my last post regarding preachers who manipulate people to give what they can't afford, what they don't want to give, what the Spirit is not leading them to give and that which they regret afterwards.

Culture Clash   *Seeing the Invisible*

So before you jump on the bandwagon of "don't tell me what to do!" let me explain something. Spiritual leaders are to function like parents, teaching and training their children to hear and obey God's voice, how to overcome selfish tendencies and how to take personal responsibility, basically how to grow up. There's a time to step back and let children make decisions that bear less-than-desirable consequences. And there are other times when parents need to intervene so too much damage is not incurred.

Insert the spiritual dynamics of giving and receiving into the equation. There is an extensive narrative focusing on money in the scriptures and therefore it is not to be avoided by spiritual leaders. Principles are not to be twisted to the advantage of leaders, but not to be avoided either! They are to be taught from personal experience.

Leaders have no business telling people to do what they do not do themselves. And people are to be taught with the intention of bringing them into a place of maturity in their generosity, faith, personal blessing and support for the family of God. As members of the family of God, we all need to pull our own weight.

Having said that, there is a place for training that sometimes is uncomfortable for our flesh in the same way that addressing sin in our lives is not pleasant. It is a part of parenting that we all need. But the key is that leaders are to train people to obey God, not man. To obey God rather than our own selfish desires. To demonstrate our love for God and others in tangible ways. To give from a position of faith, not religious works.

Culture Clash   *Seeing the Invisible*

This at times involves addressing mindsets of poverty, religious thinking, stinginess, greed, and selfishness that hinder our giving from flowing from a heart of gratitude and love and from being guided by our faith in God who wants to bless us abundantly.

What I'm saying is that there is a place for godly <u>motivation</u>, but not spiritual <u>manipulation.</u> We need to be encouraged in our giving because God is a giver and He wants us to be like Him! But we don't need people breathing down our neck, threatening us if we don't give and condemning us if we don't give up to their standards!

The tree of the knowledge of good and evil gives us the understanding that sin can be both external and internal, obviously carnal and not-so-obviously religious. Both natures of the flesh need to be dealt with in order to come into maturity. And this applies to our giving and to receiving offerings.

Spiritual leaders don't need to apologize for taking up an offering but they shouldn't abuse their authority either by taking advantage of people in the area of church finances. There is no excuse for serving oneself while abusing someone else at the same time.

We all need to walk in love and live by faith. And if the truth were told, those who give contrary to the scriptures laid out in **I** and **II Corinthians** are equally as guilty as those taking up offerings that don't abide by these principles! As Paul said *"don't become the slaves of men."* And as Peter said *"don't lord over God's people."*

Culture Clash   *Seeing the Invisible*

We all have a responsibility before God to obey His Word and to follow the leading of the Spirit. Don't point the finger at someone else if you've been playing the same game. It takes two to dance. Just make sure you're dancing with the right Partner!

SPIRITUAL FOOTNOTES

-Here's something you may not know: there are quite a few big-name preachers who follow some no-name guys on social media, gleaning from their revelation only to repackage it and claim it as their own. Just sayin'! And truth be told, many start-up preachers take what the guys in the limelight say and make it their own, not giving credit where it came from! It goes both ways and it reveals the nature of our flesh to take glory that only belongs to God! Let's give honor to whom it is due.

-Love motivates you to walk in faith despite the presence of fear. Love for God. Love for people. Love for truth. Along your walk of faith, perfect love will cast out fear, layer by layer.

-Jesus is the very Word that he spoke about. There was no distance between the message he proclaimed and the life he lived. May God deliver us from our hypocrisy, making us living epistles that point people to Jesus instead of giving him a bad rap!

-The Holy Spirit is your connection to heaven. He was sent into your life to help you walk into the reality of God's

Kingdom. Let Him do His job! The only way He can fulfill His assignment is if you let Him help you fulfill yours!

DISCIPLING NATIONS

-Unfortunately the church isn't very successful, as of yet, in *"making disciples of all nations."* We struggle to even make "disciples of Christ" because we're too focused on replicating ourselves, thus perpetuating our dysfunction to the next generation.

Truthfully, in many ways the church has been shaped by the world! We lack the authority to disciple nations because we are functioning too much based on worldly principles of competition and domination, as opposed to Kingdom unity and love.

As long as we insist on building our local churches based on our personal revelations and preferences, the gates of hell will prevail against us. But when we allow the Head of the church to build us on the Rock of revelation, the gates of hell don't stand a chance! THEN we will possess the authority to disciple other nations based on the Kingdom principles we abide by ourselves!

You can't teach something you don't know. And you can't give what you haven't received. When God delivers us from our own hypocrisy, we will then be authenticated to change the world. Until then, we will be a mixture of heaven and earth at best, and the world will continue to bleed into our life stream.

HEALING THE HURTS

-Fear is often associated with past hurt, abuse, neglect, lies and betrayal. Fear is a self-protective mechanism to guard against future pain in light of past pain, but unfortunately it also isolates us from people who could love us, bringing healing to our hearts.

Although God can heal your hurts and deliver you from fear, a portion of your healing only comes as you take a step of faith to open up to relationships that seem to make you vulnerable to more pain, but which can release the love of God to complete your healing. We need one another!

Don't let your past experience keep you from present relationships which can bring you future healing!!

APOSTOLIC & PROPHETIC PENDULUM

-Although apostolic and prophetic churches are usually enriched with grace from heaven that other churches do not possess, they many times neglect the other three five-fold graces in their midst. This could be perhaps the swing of the pendulum, an overreaction to what was lacking for some time.

Perhaps one reason many apostolic and prophetic churches have had limited success in growing past certain plateaus numerically and truly transforming their communities lies in the fact that they are ill-equipped to do so with the lack of pastoral, evangelistic and teaching graces. It takes the fullness of Christ to become mature and to see the results God intends! Too much of a good thing is bad if at the same time it involves not enough of other good things!

Leaders of apostolic and prophetic churches need to take seriously their responsibility to provide a well-balanced diet for the people they serve. That doesn't mean trying to be something they are not. But it does mean bringing in guest ministry to help develop these neglected graces in both leadership and everyone else as well. This also involves recognizing those graces in up-and-coming leadership and encouraging their growth and expression in the local church. And it includes teaching about the importance of all spiritual gifts and graces.

ACCESSING GRACE

-Grace can be accessed by faith in the midst of trials and tribulations, in the context of divine relationships and through kingdom-focused prayer. If you consistently receive grace through all three means, that will become *"a three-fold cord that will not be easily broken!"* Your grace-filled prayer life will make you sensitive to recognize and function in divine relationships, which will give you the grace to persevere through trials and tribulations, not by the skin of your teeth, but as *"more than a conqueror!"* Let your faith arise and grace will fall like rain!

MY GRACE IS SUFFICIENT FOR YOU

-These were the words of Jesus to Paul in Corinth in response to his plea for God to remove from his life that which caused him great hardship. Paul's response to these words was to put his faith in God's ability to cause *"all things to work together for his good."*

When he did this, his perspective changed. He began to view hardship as an opportunity to learn, to grow and to be used by God. Of course, he didn't enjoy difficulties but he found great joy in trusting God to make good things out of bad situations. God never authors the bad things, but he can rewrite the script if we give him the pen of our faith in difficult times!

-Because the spirit of the world has polluted and diluted the purity and power of the apostolic, we have tolerated sin and dominated one another. And because of that, we have forfeited our authority to change the world around us. In fact, the world has changed the church!

PRAYERS THAT DON'T ASK FOR STUFF

-It's possible for you to have a dynamic prayer life that is not dominated by you asking God for stuff. In fact, if you seek first His kingdom and His righteousness, everything you need will be added to you, many times without even asking for it!

Try making your place of prayer a place of.... Gratitude, Worship and Surrender.

Culture Clash   *Seeing the Invisible*

And watch God make your place of prayer a place of.... Healing, Freedom, Strength, Refreshment, Direction, Wisdom, Peace and Joy!

God is not your Santa Claus, nor is He your Slot Machine. But you are guaranteed to receive from Him if He is your focus, not what He can give you!

THE PRIORITY OF PRAYER

-Many pastors burn out because they prioritize working for God in ministry more than waiting on God in prayer. Pastors, never forget your first ministry is to minister to the Lord! That's how you access the grace to minister effectively. It's no wonder your engine blows up working 70 hours per week without the necessary oil!!

-Jesus' ministry was incredibly effective because of his consistent prayer life in the wilderness, the mountain, the garden and even on the cross. What makes you think you don't need to pray?

-Your prayer life is only as effective as your sensitivity and obedience to the leading of the Holy Spirit.

-While some are living a hyper-grace gospel, dismissing the consequences of sin, others are living a life of legalism, exalting rules and regulations above the power of Christ's finished work on the cross. Open your eyes to the grace you can access in your prayer life by welcoming the leading of the Spirit to make everything Jesus died for a reality in your life! Keeping your focus on Jesus will enable you to overcome the power of sin in your life and avoid being trapped by the religious routines of religious behavior.

HYPOCRISY

-Hypocrisy is evident when someone condemns others with the intent of elevating themselves. When this is the case, hypocrites try to be something they are not while minimizing who others really are. It's a game of exchanging reality for fantasy. If played long enough, self-deception takes root and discernment gets warped, confusing who they really are and making it difficult to have authentic relationships with others.

May God help us to be REAL, recognizing who God has made us to be, and discerning who others really are around us! This way, we will not walk in condemnation of others because our pursuit is not to elevate ourselves in the minds of others. It's to pursue God and love others right where they're at.

DOUBLE FOR YOUR TROUBLE

-"*And the Lord restored Job's losses when he prayed for his friends. Indeed the Lord gave Job twice as much as he had before.*" **Job 42:10**

This verse has greater impact when you realize that Job's friends didn't fully understand his predicament and at times exemplified arrogant, condescending attitudes of judgment against him. They were not the best of friends although they tried.

Despite Job's lack of encouragement and wise counsel from his friends at times, he chose to stay connected and prayed for them, when in reality he needed ministry himself. When Job overcame his own fear, pride and religious attitude, love motivated him to have compassion on people around him despite his tragic condition. It was at that exact moment that things shifted for Job, when he prayed for his friends!

If you submit to fear, you will be self-centered and will distance yourself from people who may not fully understand your situation, but who care for you. And you won't reach out to others because you'll be too busy throwing a pity party for yourself.

"Seek first His kingdom and His righteousness and ALL these things will be added to you!" If you do what Job did, you don't even have to pray for what you need! Your prayers will be an act of faith that gives God legal permission to bless you how He wants to: twice as much as before! That's how much God loves you!

CONTEND FOR UNITY

-"...if two of you agree on earth concerning anything they ask, it will be done for them by my Father in heaven. For where two or three are gathered together in my name, I am there in the midst of them." **Matthew 18:19-20**

When we don't contend for the unity of the Spirit, we remove Jesus from the equation of our relationships. God-

Culture Clash   *Seeing the Invisible*

given relationships are worth fighting for. When we overcome the hell that is trying to keep us apart, we access the heaven that can keep us together, moving forward in His purpose!

-Somewhere between dysfunctional relationships and isolation is a place called Normal. But what you may presently consider to be normal may be different from what God has in mind for you! We tend to gravitate from one extreme to another because we don't know what to do with freedom. It doesn't have to be all-or-nothing in relationships! A little adjustment will go a long way!

-What you need is sometimes disguised in something you may not want or understand, but if you seek first His Kingdom and His righteousness, God will let you see that the real you wants what you really need anyway! His ways are higher! His thoughts are deeper! Trust Him, He knows things you don't know yet!

-If all your friends are the same color as you, you might want to ask God for a clearer revelation of His Kingdom and His love. If your life on earth doesn't resemble your future in heaven, something's not right. That just reveals a lack of Kingdom revelation and manifestation. Just sayin!

LET MY PEOPLE GO!

Culture Clash   *Seeing the Invisible*

-I just read a post about the importance of those in the pulpit activating those in the pews for ministry.

As soon as I read that I saw a picture of saints who were chained and padlocked to the pews. They were restricted for the purpose of baking bricks for the Pharaohs in the pulpit, who have keys in their hands to release them but choose not to for fear of minimizing their importance!

The Pharaohs of church leadership would rather keep people dependent on them rather than on God. After all, it is to their advantage to give people a little bread and water for the many bricks they bake them! Don't even get me started!

It's time for an Emancipation Proclamation to go forth in the land! I hear the Lord saying, "Let My People Go!"

To all controlling leadership in the body of Christ, let people go from your selfish agendas! Release people into the hands of God and look to Him to establish your identity, not to those you choose to keep in captivity!

To those under the oppression of controlling leaders, know that your identity is not determined by anyone but God! Leadership can confirm it, but God establishes it first. God has called you to greatness, not to serve the vision of a man, but the vision God has given to godly leaders who are willing to activate you in your ministry!

Here's a revelation for you: bread and water do not equal bricks and mortar! That is an unequally yoked relationship. And you know what God has to say about that? "*Come out from among them and be separate, and I will be your Father!*"

Culture Clash *Seeing the Invisible*

God has called us all to freedom, therefore as Paul said "*do not make yourselves the slaves of men*". And as Peter said to spiritual elders "*do not lord over God's people!*"

It's time for divine relationships to function by unconditional love, not political agendas! Spiritual fathers and mothers who truly love their children and children who truly love their spiritual parents, with the understanding that ultimately in the words of Jesus "*you are all brothers!*"

Jesus said that the church should not function like the world, with a tiered system of power exercised for the advantage of those on top. He said we are to be a spiritual family where we're all learning and growing up in Him!

TRUE CONTENTMENT

-The apostle Paul said "*I can do all things through Christ who strengthens me.*" "*Christ who strengthens me*" is synonymous with the grace of God, which can be accessed through your relationship with God and your relationships with other believers. But to truly understand this statement, you have to read his previous statement just two verses earlier in **Philippians 4:11**: "*I have learned in whatever state I am, to be content.*"

In Corinth, Paul prayed 3 times that God would remove his thorn in the flesh. But the Lord revealed that what Paul needed more than his personal comfort was the grace that was available in the midst of his difficulty, that is, if his faith would give God the platform to release it to him.

Culture Clash   *Seeing the Invisible*

If we complain in difficulty, forfeiting our contentment in God, we distance ourselves from the grace that enables us to be more than conquerors! Contentment is not to be in circumstance, but in God alone. We should never be content with less than God wants for us. But we should be content in Him along the journey to get there!

-You forfeit the peace of God when you don't convert your anxiety into prayer. If you cast your burdens on the Lord and allow others to bear them with you, you will walk in peace, even in the midst of your storm. But if you allow your mind to rule your spirit, you will carry burdens you were never created to bear. They will get the best of you! And the enemy will succeed in dividing you from the family of God, and from heavenly resources that have the ability to see you through.

PARADIGM UPGRADE

-"*What things were gain to me, these I have counted loss for Christ.*" Paul the apostle

About ten years ago, my paradigm was altogether different than it is today. Certain things I valued at that time I consider worthless, even a hindrance to what I deem to be truly valuable. I'm so glad God opened my eyes to the destruction ideologies can place upon relationships and effective ministry. I can point to so many beliefs, practices and priorities that have shifted because God detoxed me from religious thinking, motivations and attitudes.

Culture Clash   *Seeing the Invisible*

If you can't identify your spiritual progress definitively, perhaps you need to believe God for a new wineskin instead of filling your old one with new wine! It's just leaking out the old wineskin anyway!

-The days of having good church meetings are over. It's time to be intentional about what we are building and doing!! Goosebumps and shouts aren't going to cut it anymore, we need Kingdom advancement in our hearts, our lives and in our communities!! Let Your Kingdom Come!!!

HANDLING DYSFUNCTIONAL SAINTS

-It seems that every significant church has a handful of people who gain their identity by associating with excellence and yet refuse to allow their dysfunctional ways to be challenged by a higher standard of freedom. So they end of vexing others with their religious spirit and weirdness until they are noted for their dysfunction and avoided or are ridiculed or are allowed through sympathy to join the ranks of those who are free to be normal. If these type of people are not dealt with directly and with divine wisdom, they will become spiritual leeches who suck the life out of others and hinder the flow of the Holy Spirit. They need help but if they do not want help they will be a hindrance. Unfortunately these people are not an asset to the body of Christ until they are ready for deliverance and the renewing of their minds. And if they are simply ignored, their dysfunction will increase in their own lives and will spread to others.

-Fear often causes people to withdraw from intimacy, which limits the exchange of God-given grace. What many people are unaware of is that grace that is accessed directly through the Lord is insufficient for you to fulfill your destiny. Yes, His grace is all you need, but a large portion of that grace is only accessed through divine relationships.

So in order to access the grace that you need, you first have to overcome the fear that distances you from what God has deposited with others. The only way for you to withdraw that grace is by refusing to withdraw from intimacy due to fear. Love casts out fear, removing it from the equation so divine transactions can take place!

-Divine relationships are priceless. Synergistic Kingdom Movement is the wave of the future if you want to see true, lasting results!!

MINISTRY AIN'T GLAMOROUS

-For those who pastor and those who travel overseas in ministry, you will bear witness to this: people usually see the glamorous side of our ministry (10%) but fail to understand that 90% is hard work and dealing with less than desirable circumstances!

Let's start with pastors. No, they don't preach on Sundays and golf the rest of the week! They generally work more than average, for less than average pay, are often on call 24 hours per day, carry the burdens of many people besides those of

Culture Clash   *Seeing the Invisible*

their own family, deal with financial stress pertaining to church budgets, do funerals, do hospital visits and the list goes on!

Trust me, if you do not have a grace from God for this, you do not want this job!! In fact, many true pastors try to fulfill the expectations of man in this role and therefore operate outside of their God-given grace, resulting in depression, burnout, quitting the ministry, divorce and in some cases suicide.

Now for traveling missionaries, which I fit into this category. No we don't preach a couple messages per week and enjoy tourist sites the rest of the week. What most people do not see is the poor sleep overnight on airplanes and less than desirable sleeping conditions: terrible mattresses, extreme heat with no A/C, mosquitoes and other bugs, spiders and dangerous critters to worry about. Not to mention the interesting food set before you, some of which tastes terrible and some of which isn't that healthy for you. Then there's the financial stress of mission expenses, some of which are unexpected until you get where you're going, and the disappointment of people who say they will support but don't come through. Then there's the cold showers, cold shaves, lack of medical treatment, bills to pay back home, missing family and friends back home, the risk of persecution, lack of accustomed entertainment and the list goes on!

So before you pass judgment on those in ministry, know that there is a whole lot more sacrifice involved than what you're aware of. Paul said it this way: *"we are the scum of the earth, hard pressed on every side yet not crushed, perplexed but not in despair, persecuted but not forsaken, struck down but not destroyed."*

Persecution for most missionaries today pales in comparison with what Paul experienced, but the principle remains: those truly ministering out of God's grace sacrifice a lot to minister God's love to others. Titles and accolades don't satisfy men and women of God like this, only lives transformed by the power of the gospel!

-If you're fighting for something Jesus did not die for, you will die trying to get it.

-I want to share something that a friend of mine told me last night that needs to become the heart-cry of all believers in these days of hostility towards the gospel. I asked this person if they would be willing to minister in nations where there is widespread persecution and this was their response:

"I believe that for others to smile, it is worth your tears. I do not mind suffering for the gospel to be spread. I do not feel good with a comfortable life while others suffer, knowing that I can help. It would be an honor to preach where the gospel really needs to be preached."

THE HINDRANCE OF MONEY

-It's a shame how the body of Christ allows money to get in the way of Kingdom advancement. We're afraid to speak

Culture Clash   *Seeing the Invisible*

the truth for the consequences we will face. We're afraid to deal with sin for the opportunities it will cost us. We're afraid to take a stand on issues for the impact it will have on our reputation and following. All because we tend to focus on our own little kingdoms instead of His Kingdom!

-Never sacrifice true substance from heaven (anointing, gifts, calling) for the sake of so-called excellence in the earth. Remember, although Paul was learned, he didn't come to Corinth with words of eloquence. He prioritized the power of God over trying to be pretty. Nothing wrong with true excellence, in fact it is desperately needed, but truth and spiritual power should never be sacrificed on the altar of impressing people with your creativity and organization.

-Don't let pride stand in between you and your freedom! Whether it's responding to a public altar call or asking for help, don't let what people think about you keep you in captivity! When you're liberated from pride, your spiritual growth will be accelerated and you will become a magnet for His grace!!

-There's a changing of the guard from one season to the next. Some relationships are strengthened and continue while others expire or play a different role.

Culture Clash   *Seeing the Invisible*

-Jesus didn't promise his disciples they could go to heaven when they die. He told them to embrace their cross so their flesh would die, thus making it possible for heaven to come to earth! Jesus proclaimed that the kingdom of heaven is at hand and that Repentance is the entrance for The Kingdom to come in your life! Change the way you think and your way of life will never be the same!!

- If you're not connected to the right relationships, it doesn't matter how strong your anointing is. You're no match for the devil. He will take you out!! Ask Elijah when you get to heaven.

REBELLION IN LEADERS

-Rebellion is often perceived as stubbornness in the heart of individuals that keeps them from obeying those in authority over them.

But rebellion also manifests in the lives of those in leadership. Rebelling against God's will, rebelling against those they are supposed to be submitting to, rebelling against the mutual encouragement that covenant relationships are designed to provide.

Truthfully, submitting to those who look out for us is only one side of a coin. The other side involves submitting one to another, which involves covenant relationships where we all submit to the Spirit's leading in a relationship.

Culture Clash   *Seeing the Invisible*

If there is rebellion in the heart of a leader, ungodly control will manifest in their ministry. If they aren't submitting control of their lives to the Lord, that means they've taken control, which is a recipe for the abuse of authority.

-Prophecy can take on many different flavors depending on the dominant grace in your life. Your insight is unique to your gifting. You have access to hear certain sounds from heaven because your grace made a way for you to hear them! And you have a responsibility to share with others what God is saying through you! Now that's music to our ears!

PROPHECY & RELATIONSHIPS

-If you seek to minister prophetically while remaining unsubmitted to God's authority in your life or being disconnected from the body of Christ, your heart will bleed through your words.

You may intend to edify others, but your words will carry a degree of ungodly control, competition and condemnation with them. It may not be noticeable to a young believer, but out of the abundance of the heart the mouth speaks!!

Read **I Cor. 11-14**. There's a reason why prophecy is discussed in the context of spiritual relationships. If your relationships are right, prophecy will be a tool to build up others. If your relationships are wrong or lacking, prophecy can become a weapon to tear others down!

Culture Clash   *Seeing the Invisible*

-You don't have the mind of Christ. WE do! We all *"see in part"*. If we allow the Lord to connect us with the right people and listen to what God has to say through them, we gain access to the mind of Christ for our lives!

-It's difficult for our Western minds to grasp that Scripture wasn't originally written to us as individuals. For instance, the vast majority of our New Testament was written to the entire body of Christ in each location, not to what we refer to today as local churches and certainly not to individuals. The NT is a 'we' book, not a 'me' book.

For proper interpretation and application, Scripture must be understood from this perspective. Otherwise, we will twist truth to fit our personal situations and fail to connect with the body of Christ on a level that grants us access to Kingdom advancement in our lives.

DOMINION IS A 'WE' THING

-You are NOT created in the image of God! And you are NOT called to walk in dominion in the earth! WE are!!!!!! There's a big difference between the two! Re-read **Genesis 1:26-28**. God created mankind in His likeness and destined US to dominate the planet for His glory. But when we try to walk in dominion over principalities and powers apart from a divine partnership with the rest of the body of Christ, we end up trying to dominate one another instead of the real enemy!! We compete against each other instead of completing one another!

Culture Clash *Seeing the Invisible*

In the words of Jesus, "*a kingdom divided against itself cannot stand.*" We can talk about "taking the Seven Mountains" for the Kingdom of God until we're blue in the face, but until we're willing to relinquish our competitive spirit and walk in a higher dimension of love, we will only dream of a day when WE, the church will finally walk in the dominion we were destined for from the very beginning!

-True, "*bad company corrupts good morals*" but the NT clarifies this for us. Scripture encourages us to befriend the unsaved in order to win them to Christ, to disciple new believers and to restore our brothers who have fallen into sin. But it also commands us not to even eat with those who live a habitual lifestyle of explicit sin and who are unwilling to repent. If you fellowship with believers like this you will catch STD's. (Spiritually Transmitted Diseases), especially if you are under their oversight as spiritual leaders.

-If the community around your church is multiethnic but your church isn't, something is wrong! May God give us apostolic strategies to transition our churches into full expressions of His Kingdom! Jesus said the Kingdom of God is "*like a net that is cast into the sea that brings in all manner of fish.*"

The church at Jerusalem and the church at Antioch are prototypes of multiethnic gatherings that reveal to us God's intention for His love to flow freely to our hearts and to the world around us. Kingdom diversity trumps local church uniformity every time.

Culture Clash   *Seeing the Invisible*

TERRITORIAL APOSTLES

-Ever notice how apostles tend to get possessive of their sons, churches and territories? That's just it, they don't belong to them in the first place! The problem comes from the intention of some apostles to utilize people to establish their identity and pad their wallet.

Truth is, in the Kingdom we don't own anything. We are stewards. If we can transcend this immaturity we will come into apostolic alliances that work together for the benefit and advance of the Kingdom. Until then, we will have limited results as human flesh is trying to control what is in God's jurisdiction.

-Many believers miss out on divine relationships because they know people by the flesh instead of the spirit. Don't judge people today based on what you knew of them yesterday. God's grace can change anyone, Paul the apostle being a prime example!

-Greater apostolic grace is coming upon the church in this hour that won't allow us to settle for anything less than heaven on earth. I'm talking about apostolic grace to breakthrough, establish and govern the increase of heavenly realities in every aspect of earthly life.

-I've officially had it with modern day Pharisees who present an image to others that is not even close to being true,

Culture Clash   *Seeing the Invisible*

borrowing buzz terminology from those who actually have revelation and letting the world know their importance every chance they get! Get real people!! It's shenanigans like this that repels people from the authentic, genuine truth!!

-I challenge you to exercise your faith today to minister prophetically to someone. Ask the Lord to bring someone across your path or mind and be sensitive as to how you can encourage, comfort or edify them. Make yourself available and watch what happens!

-The churches God is blessing in this hour aren't focused on the church. They are Christ-centered gatherings focused on His Kingdom. If we "*seek first His Kingdom*" He will "*build His church*".

PENDULUM SWINGS

-Those who have submitted to the ungodly control of others often end up controlling others for fear of being taken advantage of again. It's a pendulum swing that's all-too-common. But "*perfect love casts out fear.*"

A mature love enables people to respect themselves enough not to give in to the controlling tactics of others, as well as resist the temptation to gain the upper hand in relationships through manipulation. A mature love enables people to walk in freedom, recognizing unhealthy relationships before they get all caught up in them.

Culture Clash   *Seeing the Invisible*

GREATER LEVEL OF UNITY

-There is coming a season in the body of Christ where we won't be satisfied with low-level unity: loving one another despite our differences. This is a good place to start, but there is greater depth to the oneness the Spirit desires to bring us into, where we challenge one another to learn outside of the box of our traditions and personal preferences.

God is raising up "Aquila's and Priscilla's" who by virtue of relationship will speak into the lives of "Apollos'," thus bringing greater accuracy to belief, lifestyle and ministry. Greater accuracy will then lead to more effective ministry and more importantly, will develop greater trust in relationship that will in turn create stronger unity with the body of Christ at large.

Mark my words: what the enemy has done to divide the body of Christ, the Spirit of God is well able to restore. **Acts 2** unity that resulted in great power is possible again! This doesn't mean all believers across the globe will unify in perfect doctrine and practice, but there will be clusters throughout the earth that lay down their weapons and pick up tools to work together to reap the harvest.

In the same way that you can't possibly relate personally with every member of Gods family, you don't have the capacity to be perfectly one with everyone. But you can engage in personal relationships that create a platform for Aquila/Priscilla and Apollos experiences. You may be an Aquila in someone's life and yet an Apollos in someone else's. But if you are humble, hungry and honest before God,

Culture Clash   *Seeing the Invisible*

yourself and others, the Spirit will be free to connect and develop you beyond your present place in the body of Christ.

This unity will grant us the authority to shake nations so the harvest can come in. Without it, we will settle for the status quo. **John 17** unity is on its way!

INVESTING IN THOSE YOU DON'T KNOW

-Leaders: make it your ambition every day of your life to invest in:

1. Your relationship with the Lord
2. Your marriage and family
3. Your personal development (health, finances, hobbies)
4. People in your sphere of influence
5. Media ministry

If you neglect the areas that might seem more selfish or not as spiritual, your freedom to do what is spiritual will be greatly limited. Your ability to effectively minister to others hinges on your self-governing authority to minister to your own needs.

Media ministry might be a surprise to you but allow me to explain. Take a moment to think of the books, TV and radio programs, teaching CDs (or tapes for you veteran leaders), and/or social media such as Facebook and Twitter that have impacted your life.

Chances are, many of the ministers God used to impact you didn't know your name! But it was a way for God to teach, encourage, enlighten and empower you outside of your normal relationships and routines. Technology is a tool that God has used to connect His body across the globe so avail yourself to God to use you to bless someone today!

-With revelation comes responsibility. It's not to be used to impress people. It's not to be used to manipulate people for financial gain. It's to edify the body of Christ.

DISCERNING DIFFERENT RELATIONSHIPS

-Jesus is Lord of all, right? But is He Lord of your money? Is He Lord of your time? Is He Lord of your relationships? Do you allow Him to direct you in decisions that dictate what and who you invest into?

Jesus demonstrated for us the importance of discerning who people are and their place in our lives, including how much time and money we should give to them.

There was a distinct difference between how he related to Peter, James and John and the rest of the 12, the 70, the 120 in the upper room, the 500 at His ascension and the masses at his public meetings.

His influence was maximized because he didn't invest too much of Himself in people who wouldn't bring a return on His investment. And He didn't spend too little time with those who would receive and respond to His ministry.

Ask the Lord where your energy is to be spent this year! Allow the Lord of your life the liberty to make healthy adjustments to your relationships. That may mean bringing new people into your world or severing ties with people who are no longer moving in your same direction, or simply adjusting who is in your 12 or 70.

If God "*sets the members in the body how He sees fit*" then allow Him to make the adjustments necessary to keep you fit in His body and functioning in your role! Trust Him, He knows what He is doing!

BECOME A FINISHER

-God's timetable and our calendars aren't always synchronized.

Sometimes we gravitate towards something new because we don't want to finish what we've started. New things often offer more excitement than old things because we haven't discovered the challenges to seeing them through yet.

Do yourself a favor: become a finisher. Follow through with existing endeavors which will qualify you for new adventures. Otherwise the new thing you're excited about will join the myriad of other things that lost their luster when difficulty was discovered.

-There are more false prophecies on New Years' Eve than any other day of the year! Maybe that's because church folk are vulnerable to believe what they want to be the true. Or possibly because some preachers want to take advantage of that vulnerability for financial gain! Instead of looking for another prophecy to pet your ego, how about doing something with the prophecies you already have over your life?

Culture Clash   *Seeing the Invisible*

-You may not know the future but if you know the One who does, you have nothing to worry about!

APPARENT PARENT ABUSE!

-Much attention is drawn to controlling church leaders today while too little focus is on the exact opposite: parent abuse! Yes, there is a spiritual child abuse issue in the church where spiritual fathers and mothers neglect and/or manipulate their spiritual sons and daughters according to their agendas. But there's plenty of sons and daughters who aren't properly honoring their fathers and mothers by not submitting, obeying, serving, giving or praying for their leaders to name just a few! There are plenty of sons and daughters with a spirit of entitlement who are demanding their inheritance before their time.

May the prophetic word in **Malachi 4** come to pass, the joining of *"the hearts of the fathers to the sons and the hearts of the sons to the fathers!"* The establishment and increase of godly legacy is the only way the church can gain momentum in a culture that is spiraling out of control.

-Favor is released as you take steps of faith in response to His voice. It is the indication that you have aligned yourself with heaven's intent. It is also the place that heaven can invade earth's circumstances.

-Thank God for people who make you aware of what you're blinded to. If you surround yourself with people who are committed to agreeing with you and not sharpening you,

you'll be insulated from the truth that could protect you from harm and prepare you for Kingdom advancement!

THE NEXT APOSTOLIC WAVE

-The next wave of apostolic ministry will be characterized by integrity, not gifting.

- By influence, not control.
- By unity, not competition.
- By humility, not arrogance.
- By godly reputation, not titles of self-importance.

We will see apostolic fathers who take great joy in their sons far exceeding their own influence.

We will see momentum increase instead of decrease when apostolic fathers pass the baton to their sons and go home to be with the Lord.

We will see cross pollination at a whole new level as apostolic teams form from different streams.

We will see apostles who run the show linked up with apostolic companies to challenge the status quo.

The apostolic office will lose the glitz and glamor as those truly called in that capacity will not look to man to validate their identity.

Apostles will build churches that set their focus on Jesus, not catering to their personal preferences.

Apostles will develop community in their churches where everyone hears from God and what they have to say matters to the community.

Culture Clash   *Seeing the Invisible*

Apostles will target unreached people, needs and territories instead of marketing to pull resources from less attractive ministries.

Apostles will obey the Holy Spirit regardless of financial implications. They will minister in the framework of spiritual relationship, not dictated by the almighty dollar.

Apostles will seek to please God by releasing messages that are not popular which may cost them financially by doing so.

Apostles in this next wave will not pursue popularity, power or financial status. They will pursue the advance of God's Kingdom and let the chips fall where they may.

There is a new apostolic breed God is raising up and they are being released in this generation, which will shake the current apostolic paradigm to the core.

The wave is rising and the more it's fought the stronger it will become! God is avenging this wave on the religious system of the day and one day it will be said that *"Babylon is fallen*!!" As people are liberated from the tyranny of those seeking to use them for their own benefit, great joy will swell in the camp of those seeking to please the King!

There's a wave coming, and it's here!!

APOSTOLIC REMNANT

-I've been hearing for years that there is a remnant: a church within the church. But I'm hearing right now that

Culture Clash   *Seeing the Invisible*

there is an Apostolic Remnant: an apostolic people within those who embrace the apostolic movement today who will transcend the limitations of the current movement. God is raising up reformers who will reform the reformers!

There's greater purity and power in this next wave!! The spirit of the world will be assaulted by this new breed apostolic people who wave the banner of the Kingdom of God instead of their own interests. Those who allow their hearts to be purified will accelerate in their assignments. But those who resist will have to resort to worldly methods to control what is under their jurisdiction, ultimately forfeiting their God-given authority.

-When you transition from one season to the next, not everyone in your world will go with you or even support you. Ultimately, you have to choose to obey God or try to make everyone else happy, which is impossible! Please your Father by obeying His voice, after all He has your best interest in mind!

-Don't use your freedom from religion as a cover-up for your carnality.

-If you exercise faith for finances and healing, why not exercise faith for divine relationships? Without them, you're shortchanging your destiny!

Culture Clash   *Seeing the Invisible*

-Many prophetic words should only be released via the access granted through personal relationship.

THE POWER OF LIGHT

-Revelation is powerful! Sometimes it can take hours to explain to others what you see in a second! And when you focus on the light of revelation, it grows! That's because the Word is alive!

Meditating on revelation is the platform for wisdom to take center stage. The spirit of wisdom and revelation cannot be dissected. They go hand in hand. Revelation that is not responded to properly will convert to pride and super-spirituality. Receive revelation and Respond aggressively! Then you will become one with the Word!

-When you come to grips with your Kingdom citizenship you realize that there's nothing more important than hearing His voice and responding in faith to please your King.

-Don't panic when things don't go like you anticipate. God is working something out for your good. But you won't experience that good if you react in fear and therefore forfeit the grace of God that would've been released to you if you stood in faith.

Culture Clash   *Seeing the Invisible*

-The church would be better off if people would stop chasing a fresh anointing from others and would start operating by the anointing they already have within.

-One application of magnifying His Word is to use creativity and organizational skills to make His truth both understandable and applicable, thus powerful!! **I Cor. 14:8** says *"For if the trumpet makes an uncertain sound, who will prepare for battle?"*

-An addiction to the Spectacular will cause you to miss the Supernatural, even when it's right in front of you!

VULNERABILITY

-*"we don't want you to be ignorant, brethren, of our trouble which came to us in Asia: that we were burdened beyond measure, above strength, so that we despaired even of life."*

Apostle Paul, **II Cor. 1:8**

Church leaders need to take a cue from Paul here. It's ok to be vulnerable from time to time, to share our struggles with the people we minister to. We shouldn't be afraid to let people see our humanity once in a while. Who knows, it might just encourage people through their trials knowing they're not alone. It also might help people shake off condemnation for not measuring up to unrealistic standards of perfection that are sometimes projected by leaders who appear to have it all together all the time.

Do yourself and those you minister to a favor: change your focus from protecting your public image to glorifying Jesus Christ, even in your difficulty. I'm not saying to glorify your struggle, but to show people how to trust God in the midst of your struggle.

Your transparency could make way for someone's miracle. Your testimony could give someone the strength to hold on in the midst of despair. Your honesty could inspire people to be committed to truth, no matter how things may appear to be. Let's take off the masks and be real. Authenticity and humility will make way for God's grace to be released in your life and in those you serve!

SPIRITUAL ABORTION & EUTHANASIA

-Both Moses and Jesus were divinely protected from an attempt to take them out at a young age. But it took people responding to revelation to cooperate with God's protection.

Jezebel murdered prophets in her spare time and her threats cut Elijah's life and ministry short of its potential. But Elijah allowed this to happen because he didn't cooperate with God's attempt to rescue him from the cave of despair.

Abortion is a manifestation of a spirit at work that aims to remove people from the place of influence they were designed by God to fulfill, before they can even get started.

Culture Clash *Seeing the Invisible*

Disrespect and disregard for the elderly and the wisdom they have to impart to this generation is not only a defiance of the commandment to *"Honor your father and mother,"* but it is also evidence of a spirit at work to cut people's potential short, minimizing their impact on generations to come.

There are so many people with divine calls on their lives that have been neutralized by discouragement and disappointment. They have given up on dreams that are God-inspired.

Some, in the pursuit of their dream, have been taken out before they even got to a place of establishment in ministry and have thrown in the towel. Others have reached a certain plateau only to lose momentum before reaching their full potential.

Both are fruit of a spirit at work, the spirit of Jezebel, to kill and control the gifts and callings God has deposited in His people. The greater scheme is to hinder a generation of deliverers from arising in the land to bring revival and reformation to a system that is antichrist, dominated by the love of the world, and not the love of the Father.

Satan could recognize the potential of Moses and Jesus even before most people could see it. That's why an all-out attack was launched to kill that potential. But if he can't kill it, he tries to control it. And limiting the call of God from coming into its fullness greatly inhibits the momentum from one generation to the next.

Those of you who may have given up, know that God has not given up on you! Rise up above the discouragement and

Culture Clash   *Seeing the Invisible*

speak life into your dry bones! Ask God to connect you with those who can breathe life into your dreams. Refuse to give in to the lies that what you've been given by God doesn't amount to much. You were born into the Kingdom for such a time as this!

Those of you who have lost your ambition to move forward to the next level of your assignment, remember Jesus. For the joy set before him he endured the cross! He made it to the end when it would've been easier to give up. Your obedience to finish your race will make a huge difference in the lives of those you influence. Don't give up! Much more is at stake than your temporary fulfillment. It's about the kingdom of God and the influence God wants His church to have in bringing the nations back to God!

-On the other side of the fear you are facing is a place of peace and victory. The key to getting to that place lies in you receiving His love and trusting in His desire and ability to see you through! And as you receive His love, you will find yourself in that place of peace before you even get to the other side of your storm! You learn that *"His grace truly is sufficient for you!"*

THE RESPONSIBILITY OF SENIOR LEADERS

-I believe that senior pastors, regardless of which five-fold gift may be prominent in their lives, should take seriously their responsibility to create an environment where the fullness of Christ can be revealed to God's people as well as cultivated in their lives. This should include training and releasing ministers within the congregation as well as bringing in guest ministry, both of which should bring strengths to the table that the senior leader doesn't possess. This broadens the impact of five-fold ministry in the local church, ministering the fullness of Christ to every believer, thus activating them for their ministry.

If senior pastors give preference to the dominant grace they possess to the neglect of other five-fold gifts, the people under their care will be spiritually malnourished and become unbalanced. Others will eventually leave their local church in search of another church that will scratch their itch, imparting grace that will activate their ministry.

But if they're faithful to their responsibility to expose the people they serve to the fullness of Christ as opposed to the greatness of their particular gift set, people in their congregation will mature to the point of reproduction and the church will grow both spiritually and numerically.

-Waiting on God is no easy task. The temptation to take matters into your own hands is right there, but don't take the bait. If you hold your ground and do your part, which is to stand in faith, God will respond in grand fashion! "*Through faith and patience they inherited the promises*." Sometimes faith means you take steps forward. But at other times you do nothing, exercising patience for God to do His part!

Culture Clash   *Seeing the Invisible*

-Lord, heal those who have been damaged by so-called prophetic words that were really words of deception, manipulation and condemnation cloaked with a "God told me". Give your people discernment to judge words like these for what they are and to not receive them into their lives. Help them recover their ability to receive true words from you, not allowing their sour experience with false prophecy to hinder the advancement of their prophetic destiny!

COMMUNITY IN THE LOCAL CHURCH

-When the spirit of community is established in the culture of the local church, what each person hears from God becomes important to release back into the community on various levels. When it is absent, only what a select few or possibly what just one person hears from the Lord is important enough to voice to the community.

If that's the case, what are we really valuing: the word of the Lord or the positions people hold in a local church? When five-fold leaders fulfill their purpose, everyone is empowered to hear God's voice and activated to release the Word of the Lord in the church accordingly. Based on various maturity levels, that may not manifest in the context of church gatherings but it should at least come forth in relationships and possibly in ministry departments they are engaged with. If you have ears to hear His voice, you should also have a voice to say what you hear!

Culture Clash *Seeing the Invisible*

-For every David there is a Samuel, a Jonathan and a Saul. Samuel calls forth your prophetic destiny, Jonathan encourages you in your pursuit of your destiny and Saul tries to hinder you from achieving your destiny. Discern who is in your life and relate to people with your destiny in mind. If not, you'll shortchange what God has in mind for you!

-If your prayer life is static while your life is dynamic, there will be a breach between heaven and the affairs of your life. Not that God is willfully withholding anything you need, but when your prayer life is out of sync with what God is saying and doing in your life, the effectiveness of your prayers is greatly diminished.

TERRORISM

-Terrorists release bullets and explosives in the name of Allah, taking the lives of innocent people. But bullets and explosives are just the means to an end. What is really being released is a spirit of fear that the enemy of our souls wants to use to paralyze our efforts to live ordinary lives, but more importantly, to live extraordinary supernatural lives in the name of the true God!

God has not given us a spirit of fear. His Spirit gives us *"power, love and a sound mind."* Don't cower in fear, rise up in faith and take a bold stand for righteousness. Sometimes you just have to fight fire with fire! If rounds of fear and hatred are fired at you, don't respond in like manner. And don't just ignore it. Respond with aggressive faith, love and sound wisdom. Refuse to be paralyzed with fear. Be empowered to do your part in the advance of God's Kingdom!

HIS STILL SMALL VOICE

-Welcome the voice of God in your life, trusting that God knows what you need to hear, when you need to hear it. Listen for His voice all around you, especially through the Word of God and your spiritual leadership. But more than anything, ask the Lord to sensitize your heart to the voice of the Spirit within, the Spirit of truth.

With greater sensitivity to His voice, you will recognize Him speaking to you through people and in ways you wouldn't ordinarily expect! Take the limits off heaven's desire to communicate what you need to know and you will be equipped to fulfill your spiritual assignment. Respond aggressively to His voice and you will never be the same! All because of His still small voice.

-The beauty of the Word of God is that it inspires our souls to live above the challenges of life and at the same time energizes our spirits to break through barriers that hinder God's influence in and through our lives!

-What's cool about Jesus? There was no distance between the message he proclaimed and the life he lived. To be integrated with His Word is a privilege and a responsibility not to be taken lightly.

-Pray for revelation. Then pray the revelation you receive. You'll be amazed at the power of praying what God is saying! Without a revelation of His will, there can be no faith for what He wants to give us. And without faith fueling our prayers, they are at best only hope-based. The problem with this equation is that God doesn't respond to hope, He only responds to our faith.

FIGHT FIRE WITH FIRE

-You can't fight 2018 Devils based on 1985 revelation and methodology. Scripture says that evil would increase more and more. Unless you're living in a cave, perhaps you've noticed this taking place in the American culture and in the world as well. This means you need to fight fire with fire!

Your ability to resist temptation, overcome persecution and deal with issues in life depends on how aggressive you are to build up your spiritual strength through personal prayer and to connect and fellowship with the body of Christ. If you're weak in your pursuit of these two things you will be easy prey for the enemy's deception and destruction. Casual Christianity isn't gonna cut it anymore!!

DESIRE TO PROPHESY

-I Cor. 14:1 *"Pursue love and desire spiritual gifts, but ESPECIALLY that you may prophesy."* Ever wonder why Paul encouraged the Corinthians to value the gift of prophecy over

Culture Clash *Seeing the Invisible*

other spiritual gifts? Perhaps it was because they were flaunting their spirituality for others to see, building up their egos instead of edifying others. Prophecy, in its purest form, brings strength, encouragement and comfort to others. Do you desire to prophesy? And what are you doing to pursue that desire?

- I'm so thankful for the relationships God has blessed me with! Divine Connections make spiritual purpose come alive and become reality!

-I'm so thankful that God's patience makes it possible to get back on track even though we veer from His best for us!

-Sometimes the spirit of wisdom and revelation is dwarfed in people's lives because they don't submit to the revelation they receive. On the contrary, they attempt to control that revelation to their advantage. So instead of being transformed by the living Word, they are conformed to the spirit of the world and lack the wisdom to move forward in God's plan for their life.

SHOW SOME MERCY

-Don't be so quick to pass judgment on people when they are less than perfect. Show some mercy instead of retaliating. Who knows, maybe they were served divorce papers that week or had a loved one diagnosed with a terminal disease or something else that turned their world upside down. Who knows, maybe you'll need some mercy when you're in their shoes one day. God forbid those specific things happening to you, but we all experience pain in life and need people around us to understand instead of throwing stones at us.

-What the world needs is not more fault finders but problem solvers.

-If you see more evil than good in someone or something that is actually more good than evil, you might wanna take the 2x4 out of your eye!

-If you're the smartest person you know, well, you might not be that smart after all!

-Love God. Love People. Anything less than this doesn't really matter.

CALIBRATED WITH KINGDOM CULTURE

-When you "get to heaven" you will be instantly calibrated to heaven's standard of truth, practice and priority. In other words, you will be syncopated with Kingdom culture. You will be in for an awakening that not everything you believed, practiced and prioritized while living in the earth was in agreement with heaven.

Culture Clash   *Seeing the Invisible*

The good news is that you have an opportunity every day to welcome more Kingdom culture into your life. That is, unless you're satisfied with your revelation of Jesus. I don't know about you, but I'm driven with the desire to know Him more and I'm open for the Holy Spirit to wake me up on this side of eternity to a greater accuracy of truth, practice and priority.

-It's easy to make a god out of your emotions, justifying your behavior despite the truth you know. We can get creative searching for ways to legitimize what we want based on how we feel. But this doesn't change the truth, only our perception if it.

JOSHUA-TYPE RELATIONSHIPS

-Transitioning from Moses-type relationships to Joshua-type relationships is critical for you to fulfill your Kingdom assignment. But that transition will never take place if you aren't willing to deal with the giants in your life, who are "living in your houses and eating your food."

The reward is worth the conflict you will experience as Joshua-type leaders lead you out of mediocrity towards the self-sacrifice and self- discipline that are necessary to sever ties with the past and access your future.

Culture Clash   *Seeing the Invisible*

   -Nobody should be allowed to lead the church if they aren't first willing to serve the church. We don't need any more people on power trips!

   -Rhetorical question: what generational curses have you identified and broken over your life? If you can't name any, you're probably living some out and don't even know it.

   -The only way to your destiny is through your Kingdom Connections. Ask Elijah about that when you get to heaven. His destiny was short changed because he failed to connect with the 100+ prophets in caves or the 7000 who didn't bow their knees to Baal. He thought he was the only one, perhaps because he was drunk on his own importance. You won't survive, let alone thrive on your own! Let God position you in the body as He sees fit! He's a pretty good chess player!

TRUE SPIRITUAL FATHERS

   -Do you have someone in your life who truly wants you to succeed even more than their own success? Someone who views your success as their success, someone who is only fulfilled when those they are fathering see their dreams fulfilled? Then count your blessings because true spiritual fathers and mothers like this are rare!

   If you desire this type of relationship in your life, then sow seed towards it by being someone else's spiritual mentor. Pour your heart and soul into them, expecting nothing in return, and God who sees in secret will reward you openly! How different would the church be, and the world for that matter, if this was the norm? A generation of selfless fathers and a generation of selfless sons who mature and subsequently look for others they can father.

- On the Sermon on the Mount Jesus repeats this phrase: *"you have heard it said, but I say to you."* What Jesus is saying to you may be colliding with what you have heard in the past. You can't put new wine in old wine skins, so let Him take over what you considered to be normal yesterday. If you do, there will be a better tomorrow for you!

-If you turn a deaf ear to someone upon discovering their political persuasion, you're shallow and petty. You mean, you're gonna miss out on the 99 good things they have to say because of the one major disagreement you have with them? Really?!?!

IMMATURE LEADERSHIP

-It can be dangerous for leaders of local churches to mirror the messages of those ministering itinerantly. People in local church settings need a balanced spiritual diet, but if you insist on delivering intense messages of revival and reform all the time, the people you're ministering to will miss out on spiritual nutrients for everyday life.

Culture Clash   *Seeing the Invisible*

On the contrary, leaders of local churches need to take the concentrated messages of strong apostolic and prophetic voices and break them down in teaching and pastoral formats to ensure that people understand and live what they're being taught. Don't get me wrong, there's definitely a place for apostolic and prophetic grace in the local church coming from local apostolic and prophetic leaders, but just be careful you're teaching what people need to hear, not just what you want to preach because it's hot revelation. That kind of immaturity in leadership definitely won't mature people.

-If the first thing you discern in everyone you meet is negative, you might have a critical spirit, making it difficult for you to discern all the good things in others.

MY TAKE ON TITLES

-Never have I told someone to call me anything other than my name or introduced myself with a title before my name. And yet people of their own accord often insist on referring to me with the title they think best fits me. These days 9 out of 10 people call me "Apostle Bo."

I would imagine some call me that only because they see or hear others address me by that title. So they assume that I expect that and don't want to offend me. Then there's those who call me that because they read Facebook posts that may reflect apostolic perspective. Then there's those who have seen me minister firsthand and may have discerned apostolic evidence in ministry. Then there's those who know me

Culture Clash   *Seeing the Invisible*

personally and have witnessed in relationship and ministry settings apostolic grace on my life. While I don't feel the need to prove anything or defend who I believe God has made me to be, I do want to make a point here.

My personal belief is that titles are not necessary to function in the grace God has deposited within you. In fact, I don't see where titles are biblical, but they are culturally acceptable today. Just because they aren't biblical doesn't make them wrong any more than youth groups should be done away with because they aren't in the NT. That's ludicrous and legalistic!

Consider this: in our culture today, we refer to professionals by titles out of respect for educational accomplishments and/or positions of authority. This same principle has been brought into the church world to show respect for those in authority and to distinguish the dominant grace of God that people have witnessed.

I don't see this as a bad thing. It can actually be very healthy. But there are extremes to everything. On one side, some think titles altogether are worldly while others are title-happy because they're trying to get respect they don't deserve.

I don't get bent out of shape when people call me what they think I am because I know who God says I am. SELAH

-Mature apostolic expressions of local gatherings value Kingdom diversity in every way. They intentionally break out of earthly limitations and help coordinate a fuller expression of cross pollination than what many other gatherings are comfortable with.

JEZEBEL

-The spirit of Jezebel infects people with an inappropriate perspective, posture and pursuit of spiritual authority. It distorts the issue of authority altogether. This causes some people to take upon themselves what they have not been authorized to do, to relinquish responsibility to carry out legitimate authority, to lust after the authority of others, to refuse to recognize and submit to godly authority and/or to submit to controlling leadership.

This can take place whether one personally harbors this spirit or not. The influence can be direct or indirect, preying on the insecurity of those who either have an overinflated view of themselves or an issue with low self-esteem.

-Your motivation, attitude, procedure and pursuit together reveal whether you're driven by the power of Law or led by the influence of Grace.

-Faith in God's redemptive grace will transform your greatest trial into your greatest testimony!

SPIRITUAL BURNOUT

-There was a point in Moses' ministry when he was counseling the entire congregation of Israel from sunrise to

Culture Clash *Seeing the Invisible*

sunset, all 3 million of them. Moses' father-in-law Jethro, not to be confused with Jethro from Beverly Hillbillies, saw this go down and asked Moses a couple of questions: what are you doing? And why are you doing this?

Moses responded by saying he's helping the people because they want him to. This is a great picture of what I call the pastoral paradigm, which has been prevalent for the last number of centuries in the body of Christ. While many have advanced beyond this, there are quite a few leaders and churches that still function in this antiquated system that doesn't originate with a biblical pattern, and they don't recognize that they're functioning as such.

Many pastors today are doing a lot of good things to help people because they are trying to be a good pastor, fulfilling the expectations that are common for those in that position. But at the same time, many have fallen into the rut of trying to please people instead of God.

When this is the case, although pastors aim to minister to people, they inevitably neglect other needed areas of focus such as personal time with God, marriage and family, personal friends, spiritual enrichment from other leaders, physical health and fitness, financial well-being, hobbies, etc. These things end up taking a back seat because the needs of others tend to get put above your own when you're driven by a desire to please people.

This undoubtedly has contributed to the fact that pastors have the 3rd highest rate of depression and suicide among all professions, not to mention the amount of pastors who are

Culture Clash *Seeing the Invisible*

lonely, spiritually burned out, drop out of ministry and turn their back on God altogether. Needless to say, there is a better way. Jethro laid out an 8-fold plan to increase productivity, both for Moses and the people. I think we would be wise to take these things into consideration as well, as laid out in **Exodus 18:17-23**.

1. *"Stand before God for the people"* Keep personal prayer a priority over ministry to others

2. *"Teach people the statues and the laws"* Minister the Word of God to people consistently (the need for counseling can be minimized by prophetic teaching and preaching)

3. *"Show them the way in which they should walk"* Demonstrate by godly example how to live a balanced godly life

4. *"Show them the work they should do"* Give on-the-job training to empower people for life and ministry

5. *"Select able men from among them"* Discern leadership potential in people and carefully decide who to train

6. *"Place able men over the people"* After ample training, appoint people to leadership positions of various responsibility levels

7. *"Let them judge the people"* Don't micromanage people after they are trained and appointed

8. *"Every great matter they bring to you"* You as a leader should do what only you can do.

Jethro then told Moses that if he did these things, he and the people would be able to endure because they would bear the burden with him. In addition to 70 elders that helped Moses counsel the people, the 12 tribes each had an officer who represented their tribe and Moses trained and appointed leaders of tens, hundreds and thousands. The burden was spread out on the entire congregation of Israel.

Jesus also had 12 key disciples as well as 70 secondary level disciples who all helped him bear the load of initiating the proclamation of the gospel of the kingdom. Likewise, Paul had his key spiritual sons and secondary apostolic team members throughout the Roman Empire who assisted him in the expansion of the Kingdom of God.

The present pastoral paradigm generally has the senior pastor doing too much and the rest of the people doing too little. This common situation is tolerated because after all, that's what the pastor is paid to do, at least that's the unspoken philosophy supporting it. But in reality, God has given all 5-fold leadership graces to the church not just to minister to people, but to empower them for the work of the ministry.

The key difference between a pyramid scheme of authority that exists in the world (government or business) and the church is that church should be a family where people of various levels of maturity function together. It shouldn't be driven by titles and positions, but by love, humility and servanthood.

-God wants to upgrade your spiritual seeing to include spiritual insight, hindsight and foresight. And as you mature in your discernment accuracy, God will give you oversight to

Culture Clash   *Seeing the Invisible*

help others in their quest to see what God wants them to see too.

13 ROLES OF AN APOSTOLIC BUILDER

1. **Dreamer**- sees the impossible as a possible reality
2. **Architect**- designs according to the pattern shown to them through revelation
3. **General Contractor**- oversees phases of construction and other sub-contractors
4. **Foundation Layer**- builds a strong foundation that others can build upon
5. **Framer**- develops structure others can connect to and work together with
6. **Remodeler**- alters structure and functionality to improve performance
7. **Renovator**- updates the feel and flow of the house to be more relevant
8. **Reformer**- completely changes the use of space
9. **Demolishes**- destroys what is beyond repair
10. **Inspector**- surveys the overall condition and specific components of a structure
11. **Troubleshooter**- locates the root of problems and brings resolution
12. **Expander**- builds additions to existing structures
13. **Restorer**- brings the condition of buildings back to their former state

NO COOKIE-CUTTER APOSTLES

Culture Clash   *Seeing the Invisible*

-Be careful not to put all apostles into your pre-conceived box of what they look should like and what they should do. They come in many shapes and sizes. In Scriptural terms, there are many *"differences of administrations"* of each gift. Paul and Peter both recognized the distinctive of one another's apostolic grace.

Peter wasn't going around planting churches everywhere nor is he seen raising up other leaders like Paul did. But that didn't make him any less of an apostle than Paul. Part of the problem is that we've idolized Paul and made him an unrealistic benchmark to determine if someone is an apostle or not. Very few come even close, even in biblical times.

But there were 26 other apostles besides Paul mentioned in Scripture. He just got the majority of the press, along with Peter. Make no mistake about it, apostles are ambassadors of Christ sent on a mission with a specific message to a specific people in specific territories. When they stay within their jurisdiction they have tremendous results bringing breakthrough, establishment and ongoing development of Kingdom influence.

APOSTOLIC PROGRESSION

-I want to encourage you to continue moving forward in progressive revelation. For some, you might be just learning about apostolic things for the first time because your paradigm previously excluded that. For others, apostolic grace is becoming more practical with application for everyday living. For leaders, many are realizing their need for this grace to assist them in their primary assignment, regardless of their primary grace gifting. Some apostolic leaders still have remains of the pastoral paradigm because although they embraced new apostolic wine they put it in an old wine skin.

Just as there was an emphasis on apostolic grace in the first century, I believe we're entering a season in the body of Christ where our very survival in the midst of an ever increasing anti-Christ spirit will necessitate the reception and activation of this anointing. I also believe God is maturing those who have already embraced apostolic ministry, purifying hearts and birthing a more authentic expression of apostolic ministry so we can thrive, not just survive.

-Jesus disarmed principalities and powers by taking law out of the equation, nailing it to his cross. And then he equipped (armed) the church with the power of grace to access heaven on earth and to dominate devils! A brilliant strategy!

-What stirs your passion and also what agitates you are clues to your divine purpose.

-Apostles have a divine passion to see the Kingdom of God expand in both geographical and generational contexts.

Culture Clash   *Seeing the Invisible*

-Bitterness chains you to your past. Forgiveness frees you to embrace your present and enslaves your past to serve your future.

-Accurate intercession intercepts the enemy's attacks and initiates God's counterattacks. It always makes the devil wish he didn't mess with God's people!

-We are called out of the world to detox from the world and to be retooled with Kingdom culture, only to go back into the world to preach the gospel in every corner of society. But some are content within the four walls of the church, hiding in the pews from their true mission field.

UNSPOKEN SERMONS

-When the church realizes that we all have a place in the body of Christ and a calling in the world, the devil is in trouble. But for now, he still has us convinced that those holding a microphone on Sunday mornings are far more important than those who don't. Because of this misconception and deception, there are many sermons that have gone unspoken throughout the world.

-As representatives of the Kingdom, apostles have the responsibility to re-present to people a better culture to live by: kingdom culture. And repentance is the only rite of passage from here to there.

THE WEALTH OF THE WICKED

-*"The wealth of the wicked is reserved for the righteous." "He gives you power to get wealth that He may establish His covenant."*

When you put these two verses together, it's easy to see that God wants you to access wealth for the intended purpose of establishing His covenant in the earth. But it doesn't say God would necessarily give you wealth, but the POWER to get wealth. That power is referring to divine wisdom and creativity. You must download it and walk it out.

When God has given you a vision that is bigger than your ability to achieve it on your own, there is the temptation to pursue wealth by compromising integrity, supposedly to fund your vision. But this proves you're pursuing that vision to establish your identity, not His.

And once you begin to access wealth, that same temptation will be there to use it to bring glory to yourself, not Him. Wealth is a tool that is necessary to fulfill vision, but God truly is our reward! Seek His Kingdom first and you'll be trusted with riches. Don't let the money fool you. It's fool's gold!

DEALING WITH GIANTS

-Your upbringing was a smoke screen to hide your purpose from you. At least that was the devil's intention. But it was really the environment that pressed on you, causing you to cry out for your deliverer. It was your purpose deep within that cried out for the opportunity to fulfill destiny.

Then God sent your Moses and helped break you out of your place of bondage, only to find yourself in an uncomfortable wilderness. But your wilderness is necessary to uproot out of you the remains of Egypt within you, so you'll be able to deal with your giants in your promised land. You don't stand a chance against the giants in your future if you don't first defeat the giants in your past.

-Kingdom citizenship has its privileges whereas Kingdom ambassadorship has its responsibilities. One without the other is incomplete.

FOLLOW THE BLUEPRINT

-Just when Moses was about to build the tabernacle, God made sure he was fully aware that he wasn't to build it just anyway he saw fit. There was a blueprint to follow. Any deviation from the blueprint would misrepresent God to the people.

Perhaps one of the problems in the church today is that leaders have taken it upon themselves to make decisions that aren't theirs to make. And this possibly could be one reason why in some ways "*the gates of hell are prevailing against the church.*" Jesus promised to build His church but it seems that some think it's their church to build and therefore have opened up the door to hell's fury.

Culture Clash *Seeing the Invisible*

-Most Americans attend church with a democratic paradigm, not a Kingdom mindset. They think church is about them. They know God as their Father but have yet to realize He is the King of His Kingdom.

-When is the last time you made a concerted effort to upgrade your prayer life? I'm talking about asking the Holy Spirit to help break you free from your own preferences and personal traditions that make Him stand on the sidelines, wishing you would let Him help you.

DIVINE PURPOSE

-You had no choice when you were born, where you were born, to whom you were born or why you were born. But your birth is proof that you have a purpose. What God told Jeremiah is true for everyone: *"before I formed you in the womb I knew you; before you were born I sanctified you; I ordained you a prophet to the nations."*

God knew you before there was a "you" to know! That's because your spirit contains DNA from your Father that determines why you exist: to reveal a dimension of God the world has yet to discover! You aren't here just because your parents decided to have some fun. God saw fit to breathe you into existence so your earth-suit would give you the legal authority on planet earth to manifest the Kingdom of God in tangible ways. Catch that!

Culture Clash   *Seeing the Invisible*

-Your prayers and worship ascend to form clouds that release an abundance of rain on your life. As the Praise goes up, the Blessings come down.

LESS IS MORE

-Less is more. That means your message can be cluttered with unnecessary thoughts if you don't use a filter. In biblical language, "*the fool utters all his mind.*" Choose your words wisely. Don't waste a single one.

-The longer you live, the more you realize how short life is. Make it count! Every minute of every day.

-God is in this season aligning our hearts to His love and our lives to His Life. If we allow him to do this, we will walk in radiant Light and perfect Liberty.

-You were wonderfully made. As you are beautifully broken, the world discovers what God knew all along.

TOO DEEP

-In my younger years I would search for deep revelations in an effort to look spiritual. Sometimes I would stretch the truth to build unique perspectives that made me feel I had a corner on the truth, but I later discovered I looked like a fool to the mature.

Culture Clash   *Seeing the Invisible*

Today, I value the simplicity of solid foundation so much more than ever before. I now know that if the basics are overlooked, the greatest of revelations won't do anything in the long run other than puff someone up temporarily until someone more mature comes along and shows them the error of their ways.

-Truth, love, boldness and wisdom make the perfect recipe for Kingdom advancement in any situation.

POLITICS & RELIGION

-The similarities between the political state of our nation and the religious spirit are mind blowing! Republicans vs Democrats / Pharisees vs Sadducees Hmmmm....

-The Comparisons, Competition and Control
-The Lust for titles, positions and power
-The inability to walk in love, honor or unity
-The desire to rule for selfish reasons
-Arrogance, Anger and Lies
-Manipulation and Sabotage
-Corruption and Deception
-Immortality overlooked for Giftedness and Wealth

God, help this nation and the Church! This is why we need godly leaders in the church and in politics!

Culture Clash   *Seeing the Invisible*

-I believe our political polarization in this country can often be traced to our unwillingness to see what others see, feel what others feel and to desire what is best for the entire nation, not what only serves our own interests. Because many have felt the offense of being neglected or taken advantage of, they have become defensive.

This defensive posture has put many on edge, looking for anything that can be used to support their cause, whether true, partially true or sometimes an outright lie. This is the platform where people major on minors in order to minimize the cause of others without feeling the need to consider what they see or feel.

-Majoring on minors is a result of hypocritical thinking and political agendas. It's usually a means to either draw attention to one's strengths or deflect away from one's weaknesses. The Pharisees were experts at this. Unfortunately many professional politicians and churchgoers are too.

-Offense makes it difficult to think logically and see the big picture. Because feelings are hurt, other sensitivities are dulled.

MATURE DISCERNMENT

-The mature discern both good and evil. If you discern evil and don't discern the good in someone, you're not as mature as you think. Take for instance the Trump haters and the Obama haters. (Its goes both ways)

Culture Clash   *Seeing the Invisible*

It's easy to see what we want to see to validate what we refuse to support. (Some people today don't even have enough respect for our president to even call him by his name, not to mention his title, so they gave him the nickname 45) And yet some of these same people are offended if they aren't called Archbishop or Master Prophet! And they sure enough have dirt too! Hypocrisy.

Sometimes people look for dirt on people, especially authority figures, and once they find it they put a magnifying glass on it so you forget about all the clean spots. That's evidence of immaturity and hypocrisy. Jesus had something to say about that.

While all the Pharisees walked away from the woman caught in adultery because they had no right to cast a stone, Jesus who had a right, chose to release her into the freedom of grace. Human flesh has a way of putting others down so we feel better about ourselves. Jesus had a way of laying his life down to raise us up into everlasting life.

Today's generation needs serious deliverance from the judgmental, Pharisaical spirit that is evident in politics, especially believers. We like to baptize our opinions in Scriptures taken out of context and focus on the weaknesses of others when in fact our breath stinks too.

Some, and I emphasize SOME, of the same people accusing president Trump of racism are guilty of racism too. They just have the advantage of looking at him under the microscope of the public eye to detect it, while they're not a big enough deal to put their issue on CNN.

Culture Clash   *Seeing the Invisible*

The same goes for President Obama haters. Whether you're primarily Republican or Democrat, please choose to identify with your Kingdom citizenship more than a political party, the color of your skin or even the nation you live in.

Choose to walk in true discernment based on reality, not what you want to be true. Walk in humility and refuse to live with a judgmental attitude, which doesn't help anybody. Never forget that your sins are forgiven or you won't forgive others and hold them to an unrealistic standard of perfection.

Conclusion

Father, I ask that you cause the people who just read this book to enter a new dimension of Kingdom realities. I ask that the revelation that is burning in their hearts will be accompanied by wisdom from your heart to make these truths practical in their lives.

Let apostolic grace cause them to see differently, think differently and live differently than before. Empower them with a spirit of faith and a greater degree of boldness than they've ever experienced. Let the gifts and callings be stirred up and activated into a great clarity and a great impact in this season in Jesus' name!

May the culture clash in your own heart yield Kingdom increase as you enable them to see the invisible, do the impossible and become the invincible!

Biography

Bo Salisbury has ministered the Word of God for over 27 years throughout the US and around the world. Through *Kingdom Culture International* he has ministered in 34 nations in churches, leadership conferences, Bible colleges, prisons, open air crusades, prophetic training workshops and other seminars.

His apostolic teaching and prophetic preaching strengthens churches and encourages leaders to break through every barrier standing in the way of Kingdom expansion in their lives, relationships, ministries and territories. He is passionate about revival, reform and unity in the body of Christ and his ministry is characterized by signs and wonders. He is also an author, songwriter and producer.

Bo also leads a ministerial network called *Kingdom Culture Exchange* consisting of 5-fold and marketplace leaders throughout the US and around the world, and is the founder of *Kingdom Culture Institute*, a school of ministry.

Culture Clash   *Seeing the Invisible*

Kingdom Culture Exchange

Kingdom Culture Exchange is a leadership network based in the USA that consists of both five-fold and marketplace leaders around the world who through spiritual community have engaged in diverse Kingdom relationships that enhance who they are as people, increase their leadership capacity and exponentially accelerate Kingdom influence in their assignments. Kingdom diversity within KCE includes people of both genders, various ethnicities, ages and spiritual callings, as well as different levels of spiritual maturity. Relationships within the network include fathering, mentoring and peer level fellowship depending on how God develops relationships between its members based on spiritual and ministerial maturity.

The purpose of this network is to help facilitate the ongoing exchange of earthly limitations for heavenly possibilities, upgrading our beliefs, practices and priorities to reflect the culture of heaven in our lives, businesses and ministries. This means continually learning and growing through a personal relationship with God and through culturally diverse relationships. The goal is to see the ever-increasing Kingdom of God unfold in our lives so we can become all we're called to be and ultimately to fulfill our assignments.

Culture Clash   *Seeing the Invisible*

Bo Salisbury is the founder of KCE, but he is not the only mature leader at the helm of its leadership. Bo provides apostolic oversight but multiple leaders walk together and exchange divine grace as situations call for different leaders to function based on their expertise. This is not a typical apostolic network hinging on the giftedness of one leader. KCE incorporates a culture of family, placing a premium on the personal growth and responsibility of each member, ultimately fostering an environment for forward movement in God-given vision by providing tools to manifest Kingdom culture in every part of life and ministry.

If you are a five-fold or marketplace leader and need a stronger source of relational encouragement and accountability, and this network and its leadership resonates with you, pray about whether this is something God is leading you to engage with. At KCE we believe that authentic relationship is the foundation for healthy ministry and for this reason we don't take applications for membership. Relationship is the rite of passage.

The goal isn't to grow for growth sake. We want to make sure that God is adding people to KCE so we can exchange divine grace and together impact regions for the glory of God. If it's a God thing and not just a good thing, the Holy Spirit will make this clear to both of us. Divine synergy is released in our lives and ministries as we discover and develop the divine relationships God has in mind for us. This takes humility to recognize, obedience to connect and commitment to follow through when it's not easy.

If you would like to become more acquainted with Bo Salisbury and KCE, you can visit the website at

Culture Clash   *Seeing the Invisible*

KingdomCulture.life, follow Bo on social media, avail yourself to Kingdom Culture Media products and attend other live ministry events where Bo is speaking. And if you believe God is speaking to you about joining KCE let us know. We would be happy to explore this divine possibility with you! For more information email us at **bo@kingdomculture.life**

Culture Clash *Seeing the Invisible*

Kingdom Culture Institute

Kingdom Culture Institute takes Bo's 3 years of Bible School training and 27 years of ministry experience and makes it accessible through biblical, practical, relational and revelatory teaching. This online school of ministry is designed to lay biblical foundation in those who feel called into ministry, for leaders in ministry who never had any systematic ministry training and for experienced leaders who are updating their ministry wineskin to be congruent with Kingdom culture.

It is also beneficial for elders and ministry workers in local churches who want to improve their spiritual understanding and effectiveness in ministry. Senior leaders may want their staff and lay leaders to take these classes to improve productivity. The advantages of this as opposed to sending them off to a Bible college is continued relationship, ministry involvement in the local church and financial support remaining in the senior pastor's church instead of somewhere else.

In addition to teaching, this online school will feature time for Q&A at the end of every class, references for additional study material (Scripture and books) for those hungry to learn more on their own and homework assignments/tests. This

Culture Clash   *Seeing the Invisible*

will not be a strictly academic environment as 75% of the material wasn't learned in a classroom but in real life ministry experience. So in addition to biblical knowledge there will be plenty of wisdom imparted to prepare others in ways formal training doesn't normally address. Plus there will be occasional prophetic ministry, prayer, etc.

Classes will be 2 hours long on a weekly basis every Monday evening at 8 pm EST and will be archived so students can access multiple times after the first live class. This is helpful for those whose schedule doesn't allow them to be in the live virtual classroom as well for those who want to reinforce what was learned in the first live class. Those watching the archived classes can still submit questions that will be answered at the beginning of the next class.

The school is divided into 4 categories with 8 classes pertaining to each category. Here's the schedule for the first year. (8 months of classes)

A. The Mission of the Church
   1. Church history
   2. What is Church?
   3. Church Government
   4. Dimensions of Church
   5. Kingdom Culture
   6. 5 Fold Synergy
   7. 7 Mountain Theology
   8. Reformation
B. The Message of the Bible

Culture Clash *Seeing the Invisible*

    1. Origin and Overview of the Bible
    2. Bible Study Methology
    3. Hermeneutics
    4. Pentateuch
    5. The 4 Gospels
    6. Hebrews
    7. Acts
    8. Paul's Epistles

C. The Minister of the Gospel
    1. Discovering and Developing Gifts
    2. Establishing a Prayer Life
    3. Spiritual Covering
    4. Character Matters
    5. Breaking Generational Curses
    6. Managing Time, Money & Health
    7. Flowing in the Supernatural
    8. Maximizing Relationships

D. The Ministry of the Word
    1. Apostolic Ministry
    2. Prophetic Ministry
    3. Preaching & Teaching
    4. Pastoral vs Itinerant Ministry
    5. Global Missions
    6. Church Growth
    7. Religious Politics
    8. Writing Books & Songs

Classes are $99 for an 8 week session or $299 for an entire year (32 classes total). Classes are FREE for senior pastors who refer at least 3 people from their church who sign up for an 8

Culture Clash   *Seeing the Invisible*

week session or more. Classes can be purchased at **KingdomCulture.life** or in person at Bo's booktable.

Culture Clash　　*Seeing the Invisible*

Kingdom Culture Partners

Bo Salisbury has ministered in 34 nations over the last 27 years, penetrating various cultures with the truth of Kingdom culture that has produced 1000's of salvations, baptisms in the Holy Spirit, miracles and deliverances, not to mention timely prophetic words to churches, leaders and regions. He has ministered in 100's of leadership conferences, open air crusades, prisons and churches in the USA and around the world. Through Kingdom Culture International (KCI) many churches, orphanages and leaders have also been recipients of food, clothing, medical supplies and financial assistance, especially in 3rd world nations.

Team ministry has always been an integral part of Bo's ministry over the years as he often takes others with him for discipleship, ministry opportunities and ultimately to multiply Kingdom impact wherever the mission takes them. That's what spiritual synergy is all about: doing more together than we can do on our own. Financial support for these missions has largely been on the shoulders of Bo, as only a handful of individuals and churches have supported them in the past. Moving forward, there is a great need for financial support for KCI, not only for foreign missions but also for ministry opportunities in the USA.

In addition to many ministry opportunities in 3rd world countries, Bo has a mandate to encourage leaders in the USA on a personal level. Church leaders today to be encouraged,

Culture Clash   *Seeing the Invisible*

discipled and ministered to prophetically. Many young pastors and especially those planting new churches often don't have the resources to bring in guest ministers to help them build. Financial support to KCI enables us to invest in these leaders, helping to protect them in vulnerable times from depression and discouragement and to provide much-needed encouragement, wisdom and prayer to see God's Kingdom increase in their lives and through their ministries.

The strongest mandate on Bo's life moving forward is to initiate and facilitate the ongoing development of what many refer to as Ekklesia, which consists of various church leaders in specific regions of the earth that connect in relationship, cross pollinate in gifts and revelation, and cooperate in Kingdom activity to ultimately overcome principalities and powers that have been for the most part unchallenged. A house, city or kingdom divided cannot stand. As long as we allow religious competition and ungodly control to rule the landscape of the church, we forfeit the influence of the culture to the enemy. But as God's church unites, starting with a remnant of its pioneering leaders, the Kingdom of God gains momentum in regions enabling the church to fulfill the 7 mountain mandate and for regional transformation to take place.

Please pray about partnering with us to see Kingdom Culture increase in the hearts and lives of leaders, in churches and in nations around the world! We greatly appreciate your prayers and financial support! We share pertinent prayer requests with those who are committed to pray for us and newsletters to inform our partners of the fruit their seeds are producing around the world. Consider sowing into the fertile ground of Kingdom Culture International. For more information go to **KingdomCulture.life** or email us at **bo@kingdomculture.life**

Culture Clash   *Seeing the Invisible*

Kingdom Culture Media

To see all the *Teaching Cd's, Books, and Prophetic Instrumentals* available to enrich your spiritual life, please visit us at: **https://kingdomculture.life** OR request a Product Catalog to be emailed/mailed to you

Contact Info

To contact us regarding speaking engagements, *Kingdom Culture Exchange or Kingdom Culture Institute*, please visit the ministry website at: **http://kingdomculture.life** OR

Email us at: **bo@kingdomculture.life** OR

Mail us at: PO Box 2315 North Canton, OH 44720

Facebook.com/bosalisbury72
Instagram.com/Bosalisbury72/

Donations to Kingdom Culture Int

If you want to donate to support world missions, leadership development and the establishment of Ecclesia, you can do so online at the website above, the mailing address above or at: **palpal.me/KingdomCultureNow**

Culture Clash *Seeing the Invisible*

Made in the USA
Lexington, KY
28 September 2019